Does God Love Everyone?

Does God Love Everyone?

The Heart of What's Wrong with Calvinism

~

JERRY L. WALLS

CASCADE *Books* · Eugene, Oregon

DOES GOD LOVE EVERYONE?
The Heart of What's Wrong with Calvinism

Cascade Books
An Imprint of Wipf and Stock Publishers
199 W. 8th Ave., Suite 3
Eugene, OR 97401

www.wipfandstock.com

PAPERBACK ISBN: 978-1-62032-550-6
HARDCOVER ISBN: 978-1-5326-5683-5
EBOOK ISBN: 978-1-4982-4934-8

Cataloguing-in-Publication data:

Names: Walls, Jerry L.
Title: Does God love everyone? : the heart of what's wrong with Calvinism / Jerry L. Walls.
Description: Eugene, OR: Cascade Books, 2016 | Includes bibliographical references.
Identifiers: ISBN 978-1-62032-550-6 (paperback) | ISBN 978-1-4982-8425-7 (hardcover) | ISBN 978-1-4982-4934-8 (ebook)
Subjects: LCSH: 1. Calvinism. 2. God (Christianity)—Love. 3. Free will and determinism—Religious aspects—Christianity. I. Title.
Classification: BX9424.3 W35 2016 (print) | BX9424.3 (ebook)

Manufactured in the U.S.A.   MAY 2, 2018

CONTENTS

ACKNOWLEDGMENTS

I WANT TO THANK Caroline Dias de Freitas for inviting me to Brazil to speak on Arminian theology in August, 2015. She was a wonderful host, and my visit to Brazil was a major inspiration for this book. Thanks also to Brandon Schmidley for his invitation to speak at Evangel University on "What's Wrong with Calvinism." That visit also planted some of the seeds for this book. I also want to thank Wellington Mariano, who was my translator for most of my talks in Brazil. Wellington also read an earlier version of this book and provided very helpful comments and suggestions. It was during my visit to Brazil, while talking to Caroline and Wellington, that the idea of this book was generated. Thanks again to them for their encouragement and enthusiasm for this project. It is a pleasure to work with them in the service of a gospel of love for all persons.

INTRODUCTION

In 2013, I GAVE a lecture on "What's Wrong with Calvinism" at Evangel University, a school in the Pentecostal denomination, Assemblies of God. The audience was quite engaged, and I very much enjoyed doing the lecture as well as the rest of my visit there. In my interaction with both students and faculty, I was quite intrigued, and frankly, a bit surprised, to hear that Calvinist theology was apparently a hot topic of debate *within* the Assemblies of God. Perhaps I should not have been surprised. According to a Barna study from 2010, a significant number of Pentecostal pastors identify themselves as Calvinist or Reformed.

> The study found that 31% of pastors who lead churches within traditionally charismatic or Pentecostal denominations were described as Reformed, while 27% identified as Wesleyan/Arminian. This is somewhat surprising given that these denominations—including Assembly of God, Vineyard, Foursquare, and Church of God-Cleveland—are generally viewed as stemming from Wesleyan or Holiness traditions.[1]

In the summer of 2015, I was invited to Brazil to speak on Arminian theology and the problems in Calvinist theology. The book I co-authored with Joseph Dongell, *Why I Am Not a Calvinist,* had recently been translated into Portuguese as part of a growing movement advancing Arminian theology in that great South

1. Barna Group, "Is There a 'Reformed' Movement in American Churches?"

American country. Long before my visit, I had discovered through Facebook that there is a lively Arminian community there, and that issues pertaining to predestination and election are vigorously debated in the larger Christian community in Brazil.[2]

I had a wonderful time in Brazil, speaking nine times in eight days, in five different cities. It was a pleasure to witness firsthand the vibrant evangelical Christianity that is thriving in Brazil and to meet many persons whose names I knew through Facebook. The large majority of evangelical Christians in Brazil are Pentecostals, particularly Assemblies of God. During my time there, I spoke in two Assemblies of God churches, an Assemblies of God Seminary in Rio de Janeiro, and an Assemblies of God college in Cuiaba.

Again, I was fascinated to observe the strong interest in the debate between Calvinism and Arminianism. I visited two large Christian bookstores in Brazil, and was struck by the number of books by noted Calvinist theologians and biblical scholars that had been translated into Portuguese. One of these stores was at an Assemblies of God institution, and it had a lot more serious books by Calvinist authors than Arminians!

Part of the explanation for this, obviously, is simply the fact that Calvinists have done a better job getting their message out through both scholarly and popular books. On that score, I am happy to salute our Calvinist brothers for the good example they have set for us! But the point remains that Calvinist theology appears to be making headway among Pentecostals in Brazil, and other parts of South America, just as it is in the United States of America.

Now I do not assume the Barna study that found 31 percent of Pentecostal pastors identify themselves as Reformed conclusively shows that all of these pastors are full-blooded, five-point Calvinists. The director of the study pointed out that those who were interviewed "were not given definitions of these terms

---

2. The Facebook group "Arminianismo" has over seven thousand members at the time of this writing.

[Calvinist, Arminian, etc.]. As dictated by standard practice in survey research, identification with these terms was left up to each pastor's interpretation."[3] But it does nevertheless provide some telling evidence that Calvinism enjoys significant support in Pentecostal circles.

In any case, the fact that many pastors identify themselves as Reformed while many others identify themselves as Wesleyans or Arminians suggests that Pentecostal churches may lack a clear theological identity. While it is clear that Pentecostalism grew out of the Wesleyan and Holiness traditions, many Pentecostal churches today lack a clear consensus on important issues of Christian faith and practice, and a principled commitment to a defined theological tradition.[4]

The ambivalence about Calvinism is reflected in "An Assemblies of God Response to Reformed Theology," a "Position Paper" that was adopted by the General Presbytery of the Church in 2015.[5] The paper is intentionally "irenic" and emphasizes points of agreement with Reformed theology, as well as points of disagreement. And while it is generally critical of Calvinism, it appears to make room for both positions within its clergy. As Roger Olson observed: "I looked in vain in the position paper for any wording that would necessarily exclude Calvinists—even from among the ministers."[6]

But Pentecostals are far from alone in being conflicted over the issue of Calvinism. The reality is that many evangelicals are in the same boat. I have met a number of people who reflect this attitude by describing themselves as "Calminians." Those who take this line typically want to avoid taking sides on the matter and they aim to take a compromise position that will embrace aspects

3. Barna Group, "Is There a 'Reformed' Movement in American Churches?"

4. See Dayton, *Theological Roots of Pentecostalism.*

5. To read this paper, as well as other position papers, see: "AG Position Papers and Other Statements."

6. Olson, "My Response to 'An Assemblies of God Response to Reformed Theology.'"

of both positions. Sometimes, however, they are just confused by conflicting claims advanced by proponents of the two views.

Indeed, this ambivalence about Calvinism is even more evident in the largest evangelical church in North America, namely the Southern Baptist Convention. For some time it has been embroiled in highly publicized debate over Calvinism. The noted Southern Baptist theologian Albert Mohler aptly described the situation as follows:

> In recent years, Calvinism has been the focus of intense debate within the Southern Baptist Convention. There are influential figures within the SBC who fervently desire the denomination to move in a more explicitly and comprehensively Calvinistic direction. There are others who are just as fervently committed to prevent that from taking place. This debate is partly generational, partly theological, and, more recently, intensely personal.[7]

Mohler wrote these words as the Southern Baptist Convention was about to convene for its meeting in Houston in 2013. At that meeting, they received a report that had been prepared by "The Calvinism Advisory Task Force," which had been appointed the year before. The report, tellingly entitled "Truth, Trust, and Testimony in a Time of Tension," was primarily drafted by Mohler and Eric Hankins.[8]

Similar in spirit to the "Position Paper" of the Assemblies of God, the report highlighted both areas of agreement as well as points of disagreement and tension, and stressed a mutual commitment to unity and cooperation in the ongoing task of evangelism. However, it also differers from the Assemblies of God "Position Paper" because the points of tension are formulated to identify mutually incompatible positions held by Calvinists and

---

7. See Mohler, "Truth, Trust, and Testimony in a Time of Tension—The SBC and Its Future."

8. For the entire report, see Scroggins, "Truth, Trust, and Testimony in a Time of Tension."

Arminians, and to explicitly make room for both views in the Southern Baptist Convention.

In this little book, I want to explore some of the vital issues at stake in this debate and why they matter. I have written this book to encourage Assemblies of God and other Pentecostal churches to be more deliberate and consistent in defining their theological commitments. I hope it will also be helpful to Southern Baptists and others who struggling with these issues, as well as the self-identified "Calminians" who may be confused by the various controversies and contradictory claims in this debate.

Regardless of where we come down on these issues, I hope to make clear that what is at stake is nothing less than how we understand and preach the gospel to a lost world that desperately needs the word of life. Even more fundamentally, the issue at stake is how we understand the nature and character of God, and what it means to say he is perfectly loving and good.

PART I

The Heart of What's Wrong with Calvinism

CHAPTER 1

The Love of God: The Blind Spot of Calvinism

ONE OF THE MOST extraordinary, yet revealing statements I have ever read from a Christian writer is the following by classic Calvinist theologian Arthur W. Pink: "When we say that God is sovereign in the exercise of His love, we mean that He loves whom he chooses. God does not love everybody . . . ."[1]

If you heard a pastor preaching a sermon, and he forthrightly declared, "God does not love everybody" would you not be startled? Is not the very heart of the gospel that God loves everyone? Is that not the good news that

"When we say that God is sovereign in the exercise of His love, we mean that He loves whom he chooses. God does not love everybody." A. W. Pink

we joyfully share with all persons? "For God so loved *the world* that he gave his one and only Son, that whosoever believes in him shall not perish, but have eternal life" (John 3:16).

1. Pink, *The Sovereignty of God*, 17.

3

Unfortunately, Calvinists sometimes seem to have a blind spot for the love of God. Consider this question from *The Shorter Catechism*, which is an abbreviated version of *The Westminster Confession of Faith*, a classic Calvinist statement of faith. The *Catechism* asks this most fundamental theological question: "What is God?" Here is the answer that is given: "God is a Spirit, infinite, eternal, and unchangeable, in his being, wisdom, power, holiness, justice, goodness, and truth."[2]

Do you notice anything missing from this definition? *Where is love?* The definition mentions God's power, his wisdom, and his justice, along with other attributes, but amazingly enough it leaves out perhaps the most beautiful definition of God in the entire Bible: "God is love" (1 John 4:8, 16).

Perhaps this should not surprise us if we consider another interesting fact that goes back to John Calvin himself, the famous theologian for whom Calvinism is named. Calvin's most important and well-known work is his *Institutes of the Christian Religion*. This book is a landmark in the history of theology, and is rightly recognized as a great work in the history of Christian thought. My English translation of this book is 1,521 pages long (not counting bibliography and index)!

This book is Calvin's systematic theology, and he quotes Scripture extensively throughout the book, as you would expect in a work of this sort. In fact, the Scripture index at the back of the book is forty pages long, listing the thousands of biblical texts discussed by Calvin in his monumental work.

2. Q 4.

Calvin

But here is what is truly remarkable: *not one time in this book does Calvin ever quote "God is love."* In his massive book that is 1,521 pages long and that discusses thousands of biblical texts and discusses God's nature extensively, Calvin never one time cited 1 John 4:8 or 1 John 4:16. *Not even once*! This is a stunning omission.

Not one time in The Institutes does Calvin ever quote "God is love."

Why the love of God is so central

Now let us think about why the truth that "God is love" is so vital for the biblical revelation. The wonderful truth that God is love was only fully revealed through the death and resurrection of Jesus. Consider how the great Christian apologist C. S. Lewis explained the profound truth that lies at the heart of the claim that God is love.

> All sorts of people are fond of repeating the Christian statement that "God is love." But they seem not to notice that the words "God is love" have no real meaning unless God contains at least two Persons. Love is something that one person has for another person. If God was a single person, then before the world was made, He was not love.[3]

Notice that last line: "If God was a single person, then before the world was made, he was not love." This has important implications for our understanding of the nature of God, as Old Testament scholar Dennis Kinlaw points out.

> In the beginning when there was nothing but Yahweh alone, there was nothing for him to be sovereign over. So there must be something about Him that is greater than His sovereignty. His sovereignty is an expression of who he is in relation to everything that He created. But who was He and what was He like before there was anybody or anything else to whom He could relate?[4]

The ultimate answer to this question comes through Jesus. What we learn from the incarnation, death, and resurrection of Jesus is that God has a Son, and that God is more than one Person. Indeed, after the coming of the Holy Spirit at Pentecost, we see that the one God is *three* Persons.

3. Lewis, *Mere Christianity*, 174.
4. Kinlaw, *Lectures in Old Testament Theology*, 100.

This is how we understand that there is something about God greater and more essential to his Being than his sovereignty. Before there was a world over which God was exercising sovereignty, or reigning as King, God was love. Why? Because there was love between the three Persons of the Trinity from all eternity. If God had chosen never to create a universe, God would *still* be love.

We get a glimpse of this amazing and beautiful truth in Jesus' prayer in John 17, the prayer he prays shortly before his death on the cross. This is often called Jesus' high priestly prayer because Jesus prays for his disciples as well as all those who would come to believe in him later on.

> My prayer is not for them [the disciples] alone. I pray also for those who will believe through their message, that all of them may be one, Father, just as you are in me and I am in you. (John 17:20–21)

A few verses later, as his prayer continues, Jesus thinks back to his experience with his Father before the world was even created.

> Father, I want those you have given me to be with me where I am, and to see my glory, the glory you have given me because *you loved me before the creation of the world.* (John 17:24)

Again, notice that last line: there was love between the Father and the Son *before the world ever existed*, and that is the deepest explanation of the beautiful truth that God is love. The three Persons of the Holy Trinity have been expressing love for each other forever. God did not begin to love only after he created the world. Loving relationship is the deepest reality of all because the eternal God is a God of love! Jesus concludes his prayer as follows.

> I have made you known to them, and will continue to make you known in order that the love you have for me

7

may be in them and that I myself may be in them. (John 17:26)

Jesus makes his Father known to us so that the love the Father has for his Son may also be in us! Jesus wants to make known to us the love of God so that the love of God can also fill us. Earlier in the Gospel of John, Jesus put the point this way: "As the Father has loved me, so have I loved you" (John 15:9).

What an amazing thought! Jesus loves us with *the same kind of love* God expressed for him before the world was ever created. When we look at Jesus and observe the way he loved the world, we see a picture of the eternal love that existed between the Father, the Son, and Holy Spirit from all eternity. Because God is love, nothing is stronger than love! Love is stronger than hate, stronger than evil, and even stronger than death.

So we see why the claim that God is love goes to the very heart of the Christian faith. We come to see this truth most clearly in light of God's highest, final revelation, the revelation given through his Son Jesus. We know that God is love because God is a Trinity, and we know God is a Trinity because he demonstrated his eternal love for us in the incarnation, life, death, and resurrection of his Son.

The claim that God is love goes to the very heart of the Christian faith

So it is no small matter to deny that God loves everyone or to diminish the love of God or to fail to properly emphasize this truth that is utterly central to the gospel. Yet this is what Calvinism often does. The question is why this is so. To understand this, we need to look more carefully at some of the central doctrines of Calvinism. This will help us to see why Calvinists often have a blind spot for the love of God, the very heart of the gospel.

CHAPTER 2

God Loves Some, But Not All

To UNDERSTAND WHY ARTHUR W. Pink would say, "God does not love everybody" we need to examine Calvinist theology more closely, particularly the Calvinist account of salvation. Before we get to that however, it is important to make clear that most Calvinists do not deny the love of God for all persons, at least not as explicitly as Pink does.

It is noteworthy that the Southern Baptist report on Calvinism that I cited in the introduction insisted that the universal love of God is a matter of agreement on *all* sides. Despite this apparent agreement, however, it is also a matter of dispute. Indeed, the very first item in a list of differences was as follows: "We agree that God loves everyone and desires to save everyone, but we differ as to why only some are ultimately saved."[1] In this chapter and the ones that follow, we shall examine these differences, and we shall see that they have profound implications for how we understand the love of God for all persons.

The heart of Calvinist theology of salvation has been summed up in the famous "TULIP," which can be set out as follows.

---

1. Scroggins, "Truth, Trust, and Testimony in a Time of Tension." See the section on "Tensions."

9

> Total Depravity
> Unconditional Election
> Limited Atonement
> Irresistible Grace
> Perseverance of the Saints

The first of these points, total depravity, is shared by Classical Arminians and Wesleyans. Indeed, here it is worth noting that Arminians have their own acronym that summarizes the heart of their theology of salvation, namely, "FACTS." Notice that it also includes total depravity.

> Freed by grace (to believe)
> Atonement for all
> Conditional election
> Total depravity
> Security in Christ

The doctrine of total depravity is the teaching that *sin has affected our total person*, that our whole being is sinful and in need of salvation. For those who are familiar with the New Testament, it will be easy to think of numerous texts that describe sinful humanity in its fallen condition. For instance, consider these words of Paul.

---

2. See Abasciano and Glynn, "An Outline of the FACTS." Another Arminian Acronym is "ROSES" by Wesleyan theologian Allan Coppedge. It is as follows:
Resistible grace
Original sin
Salvation available for all
Election conditioned by faith
Security by faith

> As for you, you were dead in your transgressions and sins, in which you used to live when you followed the ways of this world and of the ruler of the kingdom of the air, the spirit who is now at work in those who are disobedient. All of us lived among them at one time, gratifying the cravings of our sinful nature and following its desires and thoughts. Like the rest, we were by nature objects of wrath. (Eph 2:1–3)

Later, Paul elaborates on the fallen condition, emphasizing the fact that sin affects our minds and our hearts.

> They are darkened in their understanding and separated from the life of God because of the ignorance that is in them due to the hardening of their hearts. Having lost all sensitivity, they have given themselves over to sensuality, so as to indulge in every kind of impurity, with a continual lust for more. (Eph 4:18–19)

Notice, sin affects us inside and out, from our head to our heart to our hands. Sin darkens our thinking and separates us from the life of God. It blinds us to truth and hardens our hearts, and leads us to follow after lustful desires. This is why Paul says we are dead in trespasses and sin. Obviously this is a metaphor, because these "dead" people are quite active in their sins as they follow Satan and the way of disobedience. But they are dead to God, blind to the truth, and incapable living as God commands us to live. This is the condition of fallen humanity.

The good news of the gospel is that God did not simply leave us in this fallen condition. Rather, he provided salvation for us through Christ. Paul continues the passage cited above from Ephesians 2 as follows.

> But because of his great love for us, God, who is rich in mercy, made us alive with Christ even when we were dead in transgressions—it is by grace you have been saved. (Eph 2:4–5)

Thus far Arminians and Calvinists share common ground. We agree that fallen humanity is dead in trespasses and sins, and that we cannot save ourselves. It is by grace that we are saved. This is worth underscoring because Calvinists have often accused Arminians of Pelagianism, the ancient heresy that denies original sin, or contends that we can initiate our own salvation apart from grace. But this is an utter distortion of Arminian theology, which insists that we are saved by grace, from beginning to end.[3]

But when we spell this out in more detail, the differences between the two systems of theology begin to emerge. How do we understand God's great love for us? How inclusive is his love? And how do we understand the grace by which we are saved? These questions take us to the very heart of the differences between Calvinist and Arminian theology.

Choosing some unconditionally?

As we begin to explore these differences, it is very important to emphasize that the doctrines of predestination and election are not distinctively Calvinist doctrines, they are biblical doctrines. Arminians also heartily affirm these doctrines in their theology. We shall look at the Arminian view of these doctrines later, but for now, our concern is to accurately present the Calvinist view of these matters. And the first major point of difference we need to get clear is the Calvinist belief that God chooses unconditionally to save some persons, but not others. Here is a statement of the Calvinist account of this doctrine, from the *Westminster Confession of Faith*.

> By the decree of God, for the manifestation of his glory, some men and angels are predestined unto everlasting life, and others foreordained to everlasting death.

3. For an excellent recent defense of Arminian theology that effectively refutes the Pelagian charge, along with many other misrepresentations, see Olson, *Arminian Theology: Myths and Realities*.

> Those of mankind that are predestined unto life, God, before the foundation of the world was laid, according to his immutable purpose, and the secret counsel and good pleasure of his will, hath chosen in Christ, unto everlasting glory, out of his free grace and love alone, *without any foresight of faith or good works, or perseverance in either of them, or any other thing in the creature, as conditions, or causes moving him thereto*; and all to the praise of his glorious grace.[4]

Notice very carefully what this passage is saying. God does not elect who will be saved by choosing those who will have faith. God does not say, "If you have faith, if you express your faith in good works, if you persevere in your faith, then you are elected to be saved." God does not in any way look ahead, as it were, and choose to save those who he foresees will have faith, or who will persevere in faith.

Nothing like that is taken into account in God's choice of who to elect for salvation. God's choice to save some, but not others, is *utterly unconditional.* Some are chosen by God according to "the secret counsel and good pleasure of his will." God, as a matter of sovereign choice, chooses to save some, but not others. If you have faith and persevere, it is because you are chosen; you are not chosen because you have faith and persevere. This is what the Calvinist means by "free grace."

> *God, as a matter of sovereign choice, chooses to save some, but not others*

Unconditional election entails "eternal security"

Here it is important to recognize that there is a tight connection between the "five points" of Calvinism. In particular, I want to emphasize that the fifth point, "perseverance of the saints,"

4. *Westminster Confession of Faith*, III, 3, 5. Italics added.

follows from unconditional election and irresistible grace. That is to say, those who are unconditionally elected for salvation and given irresistible grace cannot fall away.[5]

I will explain irresistible grace more fully in the next chapter, but for now, the essential point to note is that if you are unconditionally elected for salvation, and Christ died for you, then God will not only move you irresistibly to have faith in Christ, but also cause you to persevere, or to continue, in doing so. This doctrine is more popularly known as "eternal security," or "once saved, always saved." (It is worth noting here that "eternal security is affirmed by many Baptists who are not full-fledged Calvinists. That is to say, even those who reject unconditional election and irresistible grace often affirm the Calvinist view of perseverance of the saints.)

This point is especially relevant to the Assemblies of God because their official Position Paper responding to Reformed theology explicitly rejects "eternal security." Indeed, "eternal security" was previously rejected in a Position Paper on "The Security of the Believer" adopted in 1978.[6] This is significant because it appears not only that the 2015 Paper on Reformed Theology may not be internally consistent, but also that two Position Papers are at odds with each other. Arminian theologian Roger Olson points this out as follows:

> So, in effect, these two AG position papers are saying you can be in the AG, as an ordained minister, if you are a Calvinist, even if you affirm the first four points of "TULIP," so long as you do not affirm the fifth point! But the fifth point follows necessarily from the first four! . . . Show me a true Calvinist who does not believe in the unconditional eternal security of true believers—saved

5. See ibid., XVII, 1, 2.
6. To read this paper, see "AG Position Papers and Other Statements."

persons—and I will show you a non-Calvinist or a hopelessly confused person.[7]

The implications of this are obvious. If the Assemblies of God want to be consistent in their theological commitments, they should either clearly reject points 2–4 of Calvinism, or be willing to affirm "eternal security."

What about those who are not chosen?

Let us turn now to consider those who are not chosen for salvation. What about them? They are left in their fallen condition, "dead in their transgressions and sins." As such, they cannot possibly do anything except "persevere" in sin and continue to disobey God and earn further wrath and punishment. The *Westminster Confession of Faith* describes these unfortunate sinners as follows:

> The rest of mankind God was pleased, according to the unsearchable counsel of his own will, whereby he extendeth or withholdeth mercy as he pleaseth, for the glory of his sovereign power over his creatures, to pass by, and to ordain them to dishonor and wrath for their sin, to the praise of his glorious justice.[8]

Notice what this remarkable and revealing passage is saying. God was "pleased" to "pass by" some persons, "and to ordain them to dishonor and wrath for their sin." God's choice to leave many persons in their sin and misery is done for the purpose of showing "the glory of his sovereign power over his creatures."

The emphasis is not on God's love, but on his sovereign power to choose to save some, but not others

---

7. Olson, "My Response to 'An Assemblies of God Response to Reformed Theology.'"

8. *Westminster Confession of Faith*, III, 7.

Notice also that God does this "according to the unsearchable counsel of his own will." In other words, it is utterly incomprehensible to us why God chooses to save some, but damn others. God's will in this regard is a complete mystery to us.

According to Calvinism then, God's glory shines forth when he exercises his absolute power over his human creatures, when he chooses by his "secret" or "unsearchable" sovereign will to save some, and to damn others. Even when this Calvinist document is talking about God's grace in choosing unconditionally to save some, the emphasis is not on God's love, but on his sovereign power to choose to save some, but not others.

Excluding some just because he wants to

Let us reflect on this further by imagining a king who had absolute power to execute his will over his subjects. Suppose there were ten persons who had broken his laws. All were guilty and none had repented or been reformed.

Now suppose he orders a large crowd to come to his palace for a demonstration of his absolute power of his subjects. He lines the ten persons up in front of himself and announces: "I will now demonstrate for all to see both my mercy and my wrath and justice." He then looks at the ten people, and he points to the first man, and says, "you are pardoned, and you may now go free." Then he points to two other persons and repeats the same words.

For Calvinists, God's freedom to save or damn whoever he wishes for no other reason than that he sovereignly chooses to do so is an essential part of what makes him God

Finally, he says to the remaining seven: "and now, to demonstrate the glory of my absolute power over this nation, you will be hanged." There is no apparent reason why he chooses those he does. It is entirely a "secret" and a matter of his absolute power over his subjects, and no further explanation is given.

This is a good picture of the Calvinist view of unconditional election. God sovereignly chooses out of the mass of fallen man some to be saved in order to display his grace, and leaves the others in their sins to display his wrath and justice. And notice, these persons God chooses to damn are born in sin and consequently cannot do anything other than sin. They are spiritually dead, and utterly incapable of doing the will of God. For the Calvinist, God's justice is displayed in "passing by" those who are not elect and punishing them with eternal damnation.

But the main point I want to emphasize for now is that the doctrine of unconditional election highlights for Calvinists God's absolute control of all things. His freedom to save or damn whoever he wishes for no other reason than that he sovereignly chooses to do so is an essential part of what makes him God, as they see things. Indeed, Calvin himself insisted that God's choice to damn those who are lost is as unconditional as his choice to save the elect. Unconditional reprobation to hell is, for Calvin, the other side of the same coin as unconditional election.

> Indeed many, as they wished to avert a reproach to God, accept election in such terms as to deny that anyone is condemned. But they do this very ignorantly and childishly, since election itself could not stand except as set over against reprobation. . . . Therefore, those whom God passes over, he condemns; *and this for no other reason than that he wills to exclude them* from the inheritance which he predestines for his own children.[9]

Anyone who reads Calvin's *Institutes* will see many passages like this one. Over and over again, Calvin insists in the strongest terms that God chooses to save some and to damn others simply because he wills to do so. Calvin glories in the power of God and

---

9. Calvin, *Institutes of the Christian Religion*, 3, 23, 1.

the prerogative of a sovereign will to do as he pleases. Indeed, for him the sovereign will of God is the final court of appeal on this matter. Consider this passage in which he responds to those who question his account of predestination and election.

Calvin insists in the strongest terms that God chooses to save some and to damn others simply because he wills to do so

It therefore seems to them that men have reason to expostulate with God if they are predestined to eternal death solely by his decision, apart from their own merit. If thoughts of this sort ever occur to pious men, they will be sufficiently armed to break their force even by the one consideration that it is very wicked merely to investigate the causes of God's will. . . . For God's will is so much the highest rule of righteousness that whatever he wills, by the very fact that he wills it, must be considered righteous. When, therefore, one asks why God has so done, we must reply: because he has willed it.[10]

The view that Calvin expresses here is called "radical voluntarism," which is the view that God can make anything right just by willing it. So the mere fact that God wills to damn some people makes it right. For him that is the bottom line.

Jesus died only for some?

The Calvinist doctrine of "limited atonement" is the doctrine that Christ died *only* for the elect, or at least that he died for them in a different way than he did for the reprobate, who are passed over and predestined for hell. The Southern Baptist report on Calvinism puts it like this: "We agree that the penal and substitutionary death of Christ was sufficient for the sins of the entire world, but

10. Ibid., 3, 23, 2.

we differ as to whether Jesus was actually substituted for the sins of all people or only the elect."[11]

Calvin himself did not use the phrase "limited atonement," but the logic of his view led his followers to explicitly affirm the view. Consider Calvin's comment on John 3:16, that favorite text of so many Christians, which so famously affirms God's love for the world.

> God shows himself to be reconciled to the whole world, when he invites all men without exception to the faith of Christ, which is nothing else than an entrance into life. For Christ is made known and held out to the view of all, but the elect alone are they whose eyes he opens, that they may seek him by faith.[12]

Notice that the first sentence at least seems to imply that Christ died for all, since God shows himself reconciled to the whole world and *all, without exception,* are invited to believe in Christ. However, in the next sentence, we see the problem. If one is not among the unconditionally elect, one simply *cannot* respond to the divine invitation. God only opens the eyes of the elect so they alone can actually exercise faith and believe.

Suppose someone went to visit a blind man, and held up in front of his face an invitation to wonderful party. The blind man cannot see the invitation, so he cannot read it or respond to it. That is like the invitation to believe that is given to those who are not elect. Since they are "dead in transgressions and sins" and God has chosen to pass over them and leave them in that condition, they remain blind to God's invitation, so the good news that Christ died for the sins of the world remains invisible to them. Since they cannot see the truth of the gospel, the death of Christ is meaningless for them.

---

11. Scroggins, "Truth, Trust, and Testimony in a Time of Tension." See the section on "Tensions."

12. Cited by Thorson, *Calvin vs. Wesley*, 61.

Making explicit what was implicit

Later followers of Calvin recognized this, and made explicit the claim that Christ died only for the elect. This passage from the *Westminster Confession of Faith*, for instance, limits the redemption of Christ only to the elect.

> Wherefore they who are elected, being fallen in Adam, are redeemed in Christ; are effectually called unto faith in Christ by his Spirit working in due season; are justified, adopted, sanctified, and kept by his power through faith unto salvation. *Neither are any other redeemed by Christ*, effectually called, justified, adopted, sanctified, and saved, *but the elect only.*[13]

We see the same line of thought few chapters later, where the authors of this classic statement of faith write: "To all those for whom Christ purchased redemption, he doth certainly and effectually apply and communicate the same . . . , effectually persuading them by his Spirit to believe and obey."[14]

We shall look more carefully at the Calvinist notion of the "effectual calling" in the next chapter. But the key idea is that if you are one of the elect, God will sovereignly move your heart and mind to cause you to have faith and to persevere in your faith. But here is the point I want to emphasize now. The only persons for whom Christ purchased redemption are those who are unconditionally elect. For these persons, and these persons only, Christ died, so they alone can be saved.

The only persons for whom Christ purchased redemption are those who are unconditionally elect. For these persons, and these persons only, Christ died

Before concluding this chapter, I want to reiterate that I am not saying that

13. *Westminster Confession of Faith*, III, 6. Italics added.
14. Ibid., VIII, 8.

Calvinists deny the love of God. Nor am I saying that Calvin did not affirm the love of God. Indeed, he did believe in the love of God and said some beautiful things about that love. But my point is that some of the central doctrines of Calvinism *undermine* the love of God and are strongly at odds with the profound biblical truth that God is love, and that he truly and deeply loves all persons. We shall be able to understand why this is the case more clearly after our next chapter.

CHAPTER 3

An Irresistible Offer for Some,
but Impossible for Others

THE NEXT CALVINIST DOCTRINE we need to understand clearly in order to see why Calvinists often have a deficient view of the love of God is the doctrine of "irresistible grace." This is the doctrine that those who are unconditionally elect cannot resist God's grace or reject him forever. Here is a classic account of this doctrine from the *Westminster Confession of Faith.*

> All those whom God hath predestined unto life, and those only, he is pleased, in his appointed and accepted time, effectually to call, by his Word and Spirit, out of that state of sin and death, in which they are by nature, to grace and salvation by Jesus Christ; enlightening their minds spiritually and savingly, to understand the things of God; taking away their heart of stone, and giving unto them a heart of flesh; renewing their wills and by his almighty power *determining them to that which is good,* and effectually drawing them to Jesus Christ, *yet so as they come most freely,* being made willing by grace.[1]

---

1. *Westminster Confession of Faith*, X, 1.

In the previous chapter we mentioned the Calvinist notion of the effectual call, and I said we would explore it more in this chapter. Notice in this passage I just cited that it says God effectually calls only those he has predestined unto life.

Two very different kinds of call

So here is an important distinction we must make. Calvinists distinguish between what they call the "general call" of the gospel, which goes out to *all* people, and the "effectual call," which goes out only to the elect. Recall the passage quoted above from Calvin in which he says that all without exception are invited to have faith in Christ, but that God opens the eyes only of the elect. The "general call" of the gospel is the invitation to have faith in Christ and it goes out all persons, the non-elect as well as the elect.

So when Calvinists preach, they can say "whosoever will" may come, and invite everyone to receive Christ and be saved. Consider these lines from the Southern Baptist report on Calvinism: "We affirm that the gospel is to be made known freely to all in the good faith offer that if anyone confesses that Jesus Christ is Lord and believes in his heart that God has raised Christ from the dead, he will be saved."[2] Indeed, this affirmation of a "good faith offer" even sounds like the authors mean to affirm that everyone can actually respond to the invitation of the gospel. Things are not so simple, however, as the document goes on later to say: "We agree that the Gospel should be proclaimed to everyone, but we differ as to whether or how every hearer will be enabled to respond."[3]

Here is why there is a difference of opinion as to whether all those who hear the gospel will be able to respond to it. If God does not open our eyes we cannot see the truth, and we simply

2. Scroggins, "Truth, Trust, and Testimony in a Time of Tension." See the section on "Truth."

3. Ibid. See the section on "Tensions."

cannot respond to it, like the blind man I described above who had an invitation to a wonderful party held in front of his face. Since he was blind, the invitation meant nothing to him. That is a good picture of the "general call" that goes out to all people, including those who are not elect.

Here is where the "effectual call" comes into the picture. This call goes only to the elect, and it is this that draws them to Christ in such a way that they cannot resist it. The passage above describes the various things God does in the effectual call in order to make it completely "effectual" or irresistible. First, it says God enlightens their minds so they can understand the things of God. Next, he takes away their hard heart and gives them a completely new heart that is responsive to the gospel. Then he renews and strengthens their will, and gives them good desires.

All of this together makes God's grace irresistible for those who are effectually called by his "almighty power." When God acts in this way, notice that it has the result of "determining them" to come to Christ, "yet so as they come most freely, being made willing by his grace."

What sort of freedom is this?

Now this might seem puzzling if you think about it. How can grace be irresistible, how can God determine us to come to Christ, while it remains true that we "come most freely"? When we think of a free action, we normally think it is an action that is *not* determined or caused by someone else. A free action is one in which it is up to *us* how we choose.

Consider an example. Suppose a man is trying to persuade a woman to marry him, but she is not attracted to him. He tells her how much he loves her; that he thinks she is a wonderful person who is beautiful inside and out. He tells her he will buy her a new house and will take care of her for her whole life. He will respect and honor her, and help her develop her talents and have a meaningful career. If they have children, he will be a loving father. Now here is the point. All of this might give her good reason to marry him, and make her more attracted to him, but, still, if she is truly free, her choice is not determined. If she is free in this matter, she is free to say no as well as to say yes. Both options are available, and it is up to her free choice whether or not to marry him.

If she is truly free, her choice is not determined. If she is free in this matter, she is free to say no as well as to say yes

However, this is not how Calvinists understand a free choice. As they see it, a free choice can be totally determined or caused by God. The important thing is that *a person does what she wants to do, even if she has been caused to want what she does.* So God can cause you to want to come to Jesus in such a way that you could not resist it, but you are still free so long as you want to come.

This can be very confusing and hard to understand, so let us consider a variation on our story to help us understand how Calvinists think about freedom and irresistible grace. Suppose the man has a little pill with remarkable powers. While he and the woman are out to dinner one evening, she leaves the table for a moment, and when she does, he slips the pill into her drink. When she returns and finishes her drink, along with the rest of her meal, amazing things begin to happen. Right away, her feelings for the man begin to change. She looks at him, and finds him much more attractive than she ever had before. She finds herself suddenly admiring him, and thinking he is very intelligent, and also very charming. In fact, she realizes that she is now in love with him and very much wants to marry him. When he proposes, she find herself with an irresistible desire to accept, and she happily agrees to be his wife!

Now even though this pill caused the woman to have the thoughts and desires she came to have, she was still "free" in the sense that she acted out the desires that she had. When she ac-cepted the man's proposal, she was doing what she wanted to do. If you had asked her, "is this really what you want to do?" she would strongly have insisted that she was doing exactly what she wanted to do. So in a sense, she was "free" since she made the choice she wanted to make when she accepted the proposal.

So in this story, the pill that causes the woman to love the man is like God's "almighty power" that he exerts, according to Calvinists, when he gives the elect irresistible grace. His almighty power determines the elect to come to Christ "most freely" in the same way the pill causes the woman to have an irresistible desire to marry the man, and she "freely" accepts his proposal.

Making a sheep of any wolf he chooses

Again, it is crucial to emphasize that whereas God's "effectual call" *cannot be resisted* by the elect, his "general call" *cannot be answered* by those who are not elect. For the elect, God makes them an offer they literally cannot refuse, but those who are not elect receive an offer they literally cannot accept. For the elect, the offer of salvation is irresistible, for the rest it is impossible to accept. Without God's effectual call, they can no more accept the invitation to believe the gospel than a blind man can read and accept an invitation to a party.

> *For the elect, God makes them an offer they literally cannot refuse, but those who are not elect receive an offer they literally cannot accept*

It is also essential to emphasize that according to Calvinism, God can bestow his irresistible grace on anyone he chooses. Here is Calvin himself on the matter.

> I, at least, maintain this teaching of Augustine's: where God makes sheep out of wolves, he reforms them by a

more powerful grace to subdue their hardness; accordingly, God does not convert the obstinate because he does not manifest that more powerful grace, which is not lacking if he should please to offer it.[4]

Notice: God can make a sheep out of any wolf he pleases. No heart is too hard for God to soften and convert by his irresistible grace. No eyes are so blind that God cannot open them if he wants to do so. No will is so stubborn that God cannot renew it and cause the person to have different desires. In short, God can save anyone he wants to save by his irresistible grace, but there are some people he simply does not want to save. There are some wolves he sovereignly chooses to leave as wolves so they will be eternally damned.

God can save anyone he wants to save by his irresistible grace, but there are some people he simply does not want to save

Now we have examined the key Calvinist doctrines that we need to understand in order to see why Calvinism often has a deficient view of the love of God. In the next chapter, we will spell out the basic logic of the matter, and this will allow us to see more clearly why some Calvinists forthrightly deny that God loves all persons.

4. Calvin, *Institutes of the Christian Religion*, 4, 23, 1.

CHAPTER 4

The Basic Logic of the Matter

LOGICAL CONSISTENCY IS ONE important test of truth and an essential test of our biblical interpretation. God's word in Scripture is consistent. God does not speak in contradictions or teach things that are simply incoherent. There are, of course, mysteries in Scripture—such as the Trinity and the incarnation—that are beyond our full understanding, but there is a big difference between mysteries that are *above* reason, and contradictions, which are *contrary* to reason.[1]

Now in saying this I want to make clear what I mean. Calvinists sometimes claim that their view is driven by Scripture, but Arminian theology is driven by philosophy, or human logic. In response to this, I want to insist that what drives my argument in this book is clear biblical teaching about the love of God, and his willingness to save all persons. However-
er, I also believe that any sound theology
must be logically consistent. Logic is
not merely a human invention. It is a
reflection of God's nature, and the rea-

Good theology is both biblical and logically coherent

1. For a discussion of the difference between mysteries and contradictions, see Walls and Dongell, *Why I Am Not a Calvinist*, chapter 5.

son we can think logically is because we are created in God's image. Good theology is *both* biblical *and* logically coherent.

So one way we can test whether our interpretation of Scripture is correct is by examining our theology to make sure it is consistent. If our theology leads to contradiction, it is a sure sign that our biblical interpretation is mistaken at one or more points. In view of this, let us consider the following logical argument.

1. God truly loves all persons.

2. Not all persons will be saved.

3. Truly to love someone is to desire their well-being and to promote their true flourishing as much as you properly can.[2]

4. The well-being and true flourishing of all persons is to be found in a right relationship with God, a saving relationship in which we love and obey him.

5. God could give all persons "irresistible grace" and thereby determine all persons to freely accept a right relationship with himself and be saved.

6. Therefore, all persons will be saved.

It is easy to see from this argument that it leads to a contradiction. The conclusion, number 6, is inconsistent with premise 2. And in the case of a contradiction like this, if we are to remain

---

2. The qualification "as much as you properly can" is needed in case one faced a situation where one could promote the flourishing of one person (say Peter) only by withholding the true flourishing of another (say John), or by losing some other good that was even greater in value. I do not believe, however, that God ever faces a situation in which he can promote the true flourishing of one person only by withholding the flourishing of another, nor do I think he is faced with a choice where he might have other goals that are inconsistent with promoting true flourishing. For the true flourishing of all persons is a right relationship with God, so given God's almighty power and wisdom, he does not have to choose between promoting the true flourishing of Peter, say, instead of John. He can promote the true flourishing of both.

consistent in our thinking, we must deny one of the one or more of the premises.

What premise to deny?

Now Calvinists and Arminians generally agree that 2 is true and is clearly taught in Scripture. Therefore, both sides will deny the conclusion (number 6) that says "all persons will be saved." But here is the question: which of the other premises will you reject if you deny that all are saved? Will you deny 1, or 3, or 4 or 5?

For Arminians, the answer is clear. Arminians will deny premise 5, because they do not believe grace is irresistible. Indeed, as we shall see momentarily, Arminius identified this as perhaps the fundamental issue that divided him from his Calvinist critics.

However, as noted above, Arminius emphatically insisted that we are saved by grace from beginning to end, that we can do nothing to save ourselves. Arminius wrote:

> In a lapsed and sinful state without divine assistance, humanity is not able to think, will, or do that which is truly good. The regeneration and renewal by God in Christ through the Holy Spirit of all human capacities, including the intellect, affections, and will, is required for humanity to understand, esteem, consider, will, and perform that which is truly good.[3]

Anyone who has read Arminius himself knows that he believed salvation was thoroughly a gift of God's grace. But again, the issue is whether grace is *irresistible*. Here is how Arminius put that point.

> The entire controversy can be reduced to answering this question, "Is the grace of God an irresistible force?" In other words, the controversy does not relate to those

---

3. Arminius, *Arminius and his Declaration of Sentiments*, 140.

actions or operations that may properly be ascribed to grace, for I acknowledge and ascribe to grace as many of those actions or operations as any man has ever done. No, the controversy relates solely to the mode of operation, whether it be irresistible or not. I believe that Scripture teaches that many persons resist the Holy Spirit and reject the grace offered.[4]

Arminius cited a number of biblical texts that teach that grace is resistible. Here are a few of them.

- "You stiff necked people with uncircumcised hearts and ears. You are just like your fathers: You always resist the Holy Spirit" (Acts 7:51).

- "As God's fellow workers, we urge you not to receive the grace of God in vain" (2 Cor 6:1; cf. Heb 12:15)

- "O Jerusalem, O Jerusalem, you who kill the prophets and stone those sent to you, how often have a I longed to gather your children together, as a hen gathers her chicks under her wings, but you were not willing" (Matt 23:37).

The entire controversy can be reduced to answering this question, "Is the grace of God an irresistible force?"

- "But the Pharisees and experts of the law rejected God's purpose for themselves because they had not been baptized by John" (Luke 7:30).

These are some of the texts that support the doctrine of prevenient grace. This is the grace Arminians believe God gives to us to empower us to exercise faith and be saved. While this grace *enables* us to exercise faith in Christ, it does not *determine* or cause us to do so. We must freely respond to God's grace rather than resist it. Christ made clear in Matthew 23:37 that he had a deep love for

4. Ibid., 141.

his people, like a mother hen has for her chicks. But sadly, he said that they "were not willing" to come to him and accept his love. The fault was entirely theirs. It was not in any way because he simply chose to leave them in their sins.

But what's a Calvinist to do?

So the Arminian has a clear answer when asked which of the premises of this argument he rejects. But what about the Calvinist? It seems clear that no biblical Christian could deny premise number 4. Human beings are made in the image of God, and our very nature is such that we can only find true fulfillment in knowing and loving God. That is what it means to be a human being. *The Shorter Catechism* of the *Westminster Confession of Faith* famously makes this point in the very first question.

> Question: What is the chief end of man?
> Answer: The chief end of man is to glorify God and enjoy him forever.

We can only experience the true enjoyment for which we were created if we know and love God. For fallen man, this means we can only achieve this end through "a saving relationship in which we love and obey him."

What about premise number 3? This also seems to be clearly true. Consider these words of Scripture.

> This is how we know what love is: Jesus Christ laid down his life for us. And we ought to lay down our lives for our brothers. If anyone has material possessions and sees his brother in need but has no pity on him, how can the love of God be in him? Dear children, let us not love with words or tongue but with actions and in truth. (1 John 3:16–18)

Love is more than a word! It is not enough to profess to love if we never show it in our actions. If we truly love, we are required to act to promote the true well-being and flourishing of those we say we love.

If the Calvinist does not want to deny premise 3, the only option left is to deny premise 1. And now I think we are in a position to fully understand Arthur Pink's statement that I quoted at the beginning of this book. I would suggest that Pink understands the logic of Calvinism perfectly and is willing to be completely consistent with his Calvinist convictions.

In other words, a fully consistent Calvinist who truly understands unconditional election, limited atonement, and irresistible grace will deny that God loves all persons. Why? Because according to Calvinism, God *could* give irresistible grace to all persons, and cause all of them to come to Christ "most freely" (as the Calvinist defines freedom). But he chooses not to do so, and as an expression of his sovereign power, he chooses to damn some persons he could easily save if he wanted to. Recall again Calvin's words: "Therefore, those whom God passes over, he condemns; *and this for no other reason than that he wills to exclude them* from the inheritance which he predestines for his own children." God excludes some people from salvation "for no other reason than that he wills to exclude them."

A truly consistent Calvinist . . . will deny that God loves all persons

It seems clear that God does not love these persons since God chooses not to save them (for the simple reason that he does not desire to do so), and consequently Christ was not sent to die for them. This is stark, forthright, unvarnished

If God does not give the unconverted his irresistible grace, his "salvific stance" toward them is a hollow gesture

Calvinism. It is no wonder Calvin never quoted the beautiful biblical truth that "God is love" even one time in his *Institutes*. He was so mesmerized by God's sovereign power that he could not see God's love for all persons.

CHAPTER 5

Calvinist Love for All?

MOST CALVINISTS ARE NOT as consistent and straightforward as Arthur Pink. Most are not so forthright in expressing the belief that God does not love everyone. In fact, as noted in an earlier chapter, many Calvinists are emphatic in insisting that God *does* love everyone. Often they are just inconsistent or have simply not thought through the implications of their theology. When this is so, Calvinists typically make claims that are deeply at odds with their distinctive doctrines of unconditional election, limited atonement, and irresistible grace.

Sometimes, however, Calvinists are aware that their theology calls into question God's love for everyone, and they make some clever moves to insist that he does in fact love all persons. D. A. Carson is a Calvinist New Testament scholar, and he is a good example of what I am talking about. He shares his experience as follows: "When I have preached or lectured in Reformed [Calvinist] circles, I have often been asked the question, 'Do you feel free to tell unbelievers that God loves them?'"[1]

"Do you feel free to tell unbelievers that God loves them?"

1. Carson, *The Difficult Doctrine of the Love of God*, 78.

Notice, Carson does not say he is asked this question occasionally or once in a while. He says he has *often* been asked the question by young Calvinist pastors. The reason is obvious. This is a perfectly natural question for a Calvinist pastor to ask.

Think about that for a moment. Here are young pastors who wonder whether they can even tell unbelievers that God loves them! What does it say about a theological system if many of those who believe it doubt whether God loves unbelievers? But more importantly, notice that this issue is not simply an academic question to be debated by scholars and theologians. What is at stake is the very nature of the gospel we preach. Do we have good news for everyone? Is there a message of hope for all persons? Can we honestly preach to *all* unbelievers that God loves them?

A surprising answer to a surprising question

But what is most interesting, and revealing here is how Carson answers the question. Here is his answer to this question from young Calvinist pastors: "*Of course* I tell the unconverted that God loves them."[2]

Now if you have followed the discussion so far, and especially the logical argument of the last chapter, you should at least be puzzled at Carson's answer. Since God unconditionally chooses not to save some people, how can he love those people who are not among his chosen elect?

The key to answering this question is to know that Carson distinguishes several senses of love in the Bible. Three of these are especially relevant to understanding how he can tell the unconverted that God loves them. Here they are.

1. God's providential love over all that he has made.

2. God's salvific stance toward his fallen world.

2. Ibid., 78.

38

3. God's particular, effective, selecting love toward his elect.[3]

So how can Carson tell the unconverted that God loves them? Well, he can do so because he believes God loves all people, believers as well as unbelievers, *at least in the first two senses.*

"Love" for the non-elect

Let us consider this account of love more carefully. First, God's providential love is shown in the fact that God has not only made a beautiful world, but one in which our physical needs can be met. There is food available in this world, and water to drink, and God "causes his sun to rise on the evil and the good, and sends rain on the righteous and the unrighteous" (Matt 5:45). So God loves the unconverted in the sense that they can enjoy the blessings of God's good world and the things it provides to meet our physical needs.

Second, God also loves the unconverted in the sense that he takes a "salvific stance" toward them. What does this mean? Well, it means that God commands all persons to repent, and invites all people to believe the gospel and be saved. In other words, this is essentially the "general call" of the gospel that goes out to all persons, the non-elect as well as the elect.

Unfortunately however, Carson does not believe God loves all the unconverted in the third sense above. This kind of love applies only to those who are unconditionally elect. So here is the problem for Carson's claim that God loves the unconverted. If any of them are not elect, they cannot possibly respond positively to God command to repent and believe the gospel. Without the "effectual call" no one is able to answer the "general call" of the gospel. If God does not give the unconverted his irresistible grace,

---

3. Ibid., 16–18. In Carson's book, these are numbers 2–4.

his "salvific stance" toward them is a hollow gesture. Again, it is like a holding an invitation to a party in front of a blind man.[4]

What about God's providential blessings in the form of provision for food, rain, water, and so on? Does this show that God loves the unconverted? Unfortunately not, if those unconverted are not among God's unconditionally elect.

Consider an analogy. Suppose a scientist needs some perfectly healthy twenty-five-year-old persons for some medical experiments he wants to perform that will be extremely painful for these persons, and will cause them to die an agonizing death. To get these persons, he acquires ten children that he raises in ideal circumstances. These children have no idea of his plans for them and they are repeatedly told the scientist loves them. He gives them the best of treatment as he raises them. They are fed delicious and nutritious food. They wear the best and most stylish clothes, they live in beautiful homes and drive new cars when they are old enough to drive. They receive the best medical care, and have numerous recreational and social opportunities. In short, they have every advantage and benefit that money can buy . . . until they are twenty five years old, at which time they are subjected to those painful experiments that will lead to a horrible death.

Now here is the question: could anyone say with a straight face that this scientist *loved* these children? It is obvious he does not love them, despite the fact that he provides for them lavishly for the first twenty-five years of their lives. It is clear he does not love them, because he does not care about their true well-being or

4. Calvinists might point out that traditional Arminians have a parallel problem because God invites people to believe the gospel when he foreknows they will not do so. While there is a certain parallel here, there are also crucial differences. According to Arminians, God gives grace to all persons, which truly enables them to respond and accept the gospel. Moreover, God sincerely desires all to accept his grace. This makes clear that any who reject the gospel do so entirely of their own free will, and they could have done otherwise. For more on this, see pp. 68–71 below.

promote their ultimate flourishing. He cares only for their *temporary* flourishing so he can use them for his experiments.

So the main point is clear. If God loves some people only in the first two senses listed above, but not in the third, his "love" is meaningless. Temporal blessings are not nearly enough to show that God loves the unconverted if God has chosen to withhold his irresistible grace, leaving them dead in sins, and thereby consigning them to the misery of eternal damnation in hell. Jesus reminded us quite clearly that temporal blessings without eternal life are worth nothing. "What good will it be for a man if he gains the whole world, yet forfeits his soul?" (Matt 16:26).

It is clear he does not love them, because he does not care about their true well-being or promote their ultimate flourishing

Back to the logic of the matter

Let us return to the logical argument of the previous chapter.

1. God truly loves all persons.

2. Not all persons will be saved.

3. Truly to love someone is to desire their well-being and to promote their true flourishing as much as you properly can.

4. The well-being and true flourishing of all persons is to be found in a right relationship with God, a saving relationship in which we love and obey him.

5. God could give all persons "irresistible grace" and thereby determine all persons to freely accept a right relationship with himself and be saved.

6. Therefore, all persons will be saved.

Some Calvinists, you will recall, deny premise 1, but Carson, wants to affirm premise 1. It appears, however, that he denies premise 3. He believes God can love the unconverted even if he does not do all he can to promote their true well-being and ultimate flourishing. For he could do so by giving them irresistible grace and causing them to "freely" accept Christ and a right relationship with God. However, those who are not elect do not receive irresistible grace, so they cannot possibly receive the one thing they need most for their true well-being and ultimate flourishing.

Suppose now that Carson was forthright in explaining what he means when he tells the unconverted that God loves them. Suppose he said something like the following.

> I do not know whether or not you are one of the elect that God loves with his "particular, effective, selective love." For all I know, God has chosen to pass you by rather than give you his irresistible grace, which you need to be saved. If so, you are headed for eternal hell and there is no possibility you can be saved. Still, God loves you because he has provided food and water for you to eat, and rain to grow your garden. Also, God shows you his love by inviting you to accept Jesus, even though it will be impossible for you to accept the invitation if you are not one of the unconditionally elect.

If Carson spoke like this, and openly and honestly told the unconverted what he meant when he assures them that God loves them, would anyone take it seriously? It's hard to imagine they would. So Carson is guilty of equivocating on the word "love," to say the least, by using it in a misleading way when he tells the unconverted that God loves them. But this is the sort of thing Calvinists have to resort to if they do not want to deny outright that God truly loves everyone.

God has other goals

But Calvinists sometimes make another move in an effort to say God loves the people he has sovereignly chosen not to save. A well-known contemporary proponent of this move is the famous Calvinist pastor John Piper. Piper insists that God truly and deeply loves the people he has chosen for damnation. Even though God has compassion on these people, he cannot save them because he has other purposes he must accomplish, and these purposes are simply incompatible with saving those he chooses to damn. In other words, God has higher purposes and goals that prevent him from saving all persons. What this means is that there are "two wills" in God concerning those who are damned. He wills to save them in one sense, but in another sense he wills to damn them in order to accomplish his higher purposes.

So going back to the logical argument above, Piper would apparently deny premise 5. Contrary to that premise, God actually *cannot* give all persons irresistible grace, and cause all persons to freely accept a right relationship with himself and be saved. However, the reason he cannot do so has nothing to do with human freedom. The reason he cannot save all persons is because he has other purposes that are incompatible with doing so.

Why must God damn?

So what is this higher purpose God has that prevents him from saving those he chooses to damn? Here is Piper's answer to this question.

For Piper, God must damn some people to hell forever in order to fully glorify himself in his creation

> The answer the Reformed give is that the greater value is the manifestation of the full range of God's glory in wrath and mercy (Romans 9:22–23) and the

humbling of man so he enjoys giving all credit to God
for his salvation (I Cor. 1:29).[5]

Piper's view hinges on a claim we can fully agree with,
namely, that God is true to himself. Indeed, he would not be God
if he were not true to himself. But for Piper, this requires that
God must fully display his wrath, for if he did not fully display
his wrath, he would not be fully glorified. And for him to fully
display his wrath, some persons must be damned forever. So for
Piper, God *must* damn some people to hell forever in order to
fully glorify himself in his creation. We can spell out the logic of
Piper's view as follows.

1. God is true to himself.

2. If God is true to himself, his full glory must be displayed.

3. If God's full glory must be displayed, his wrath must be
   fully displayed.

4. If God's wrath must be fully displayed, there must be evil
   persons who are eternally damned.

5. If God is true to himself, there must be persons who are
   eternally damned.

Now again, what is remarkable about Piper's position is
his claim that God has true compassion on those he chooses to
damn. He loves them and feels bad for them, as it were, but given
that his higher goal of glorifying himself requires him to damn
some people, they must be damned forever in hell. Piper puts it
like this.

> God has a real and deep compassion for perishing sin-
> ners. . . . God's expressions of pity and his entreaties
> have heart in them. There is a genuine inclination in
> God's heart to spare those who have committed treason
> against his kingdom. . . . In his great and mysterious

5. Piper, *Does God Desire All to Be Saved?* 39.

heart, there are kinds of longings and desires that are real—they tell us something true about his character. Yet not all of these longings govern his actions.[6]

So God's heart is deeply divided, according to Piper. He determines some to sin by his sovereign will, and then damns them to hell for the very sins he has determined them to commit. Obviously, their freedom does not keep him from saving them because God could give any of them his "irresistible grace," which would cause them to believe the gospel and come to Christ "most freely." The reason God cannot save them is that he has "higher" goals that prevent him from doing so. He must fully glorify himself, and for Piper, that requires him to damn many people to hell forever.

Does God actually need some people to go to hell?

Now Piper's appeal to the glory of God sounds very pious. However, his position raises some troubling questions. Does God *actually need* eternal hell to glorify himself? Is the true glory of the eternal God such that it could not be fully displayed to his creation unless he chose to damn some persons?

Now the doctrine of hell is a difficult one regardless of our theology. But here is one big question that opens a large window into the heart of any theological system: why, according to your theology, do some persons go to hell? Why are some persons separated from the love of God and lost forever? Does your theology say that it is *necessary that some persons must go to hell?* Or is it possible, in principle, that all could be saved? Did Jesus die for all, and make it possible for all to be saved, so that those who go to hell do so *entirely by their own choice?* Or does God sovereignly choose to damn some as a necessary measure to fully display his glory?

6. Ibid., 48–49.

45

Does God Love Everyone?

Despite Piper's claim that he is only concerned for the glory of God, his theology severely diminishes the love of God, and thereby casts a dark shadow over his true glory. To see this, consider this analogy by Thomas McCall that he wrote in order to illustrate the problems in Piper's theology.

> *Despite Piper's claim that he is only concerned for the glory of God, his theology severely diminishes the love of God, and thereby casts a dark shadow over his true glory*

Imagine a parent who is able to control each and every action of his children, and furthermore, is able to do so by controlling their thoughts and inclinations. He is thus able to determine each and all actions taken by those children. He is also able to guarantee that they desire to do everything that they do, and this is exactly what he does. He puts them in a special playroom that contains not only toys but also gasoline and matches, and then gives them explicit instructions (with severe warnings) to avoid touching the gasoline and matches. Stepping out of sight, he determines that the children indeed begin to play with the matches. When the playroom is ablaze and the situation desperate, he rushes in to save them (well, some of them). He breaks through the wall, grabs three of the seven children, and carries them to safety. When the rescued children calm down, they ask about their four siblings. They want to know about the others trapped inside, awaiting their inevitable fate. More importantly, they want to know if he can do something to rescue them as well.

When they ask about the situation, their father tells them that this tragic occurrence had been determined by him, and indeed, that it was a smashing success—it had worked out in exact accordance with his plan. He then reminds them of his instructions and warnings, and he reminds them further that they willingly violated his commands. They should be grateful for their rescue, and they should understand that the others got what they deserved. When they begin to sob, he weeps with them; he tells them that he too has compassion on the doomed children (indeed, the compassion of the children for their siblings only dimly reflects his own). The children are puzzled by this, and one wants to know why such a compassionate father does not rescue the others (when it is clearly within his power to do so). His answer is this: this has happened so that everyone could see how smart he is (for being able to know how to do all this), how powerful he is (for being able to control everything and then effectively rescue them), how merciful he is (for rescuing the children who broke his rules), and how just he is (for leaving the others to their fate in the burning playroom). And, he says, "This is the righteous thing for me to do, because it allows me to look as good as I should look."[7]

McCall's parable of a father who would choose to leave some of his children to burn "because it allows [him] to look as good as [he] should look" is poignant and even disturbing. But what is really disturbing here is that the story is an accurate portrayal of how many Calvinists view God.

Indeed, the parable is particularly poignant in light of a passage I read from Piper several years ago, and have never forgotten. In this passage, Piper was spelling out his view of how a sovereign God loves, and he made the point very personal by talking about his own children. He shared how he hoped and prayed that his own sons would have faith in Christ and even join him in Christian ministry. He then went on as follows.

> But I am not ignorant that God may not have chosen my sons for his sons. And, though I think I would give my life for their salvation, if they should be lost to me, I

---

7. McCall, "We Believe in God's Sovereign Goodness: A Rejoinder to John Piper," 241–42.

would not rail against the Almighty. He is God. I am but a man. The potter has absolute rights over the clay. Mine is to bow before his unimpeachable character and believe that the Judge of all the earth has ever and always will do right.[8]

Ironically, it even seems Piper is more certain of his own desire to see his children saved than he is that God wills their salvation

Again, what is striking here is the notion that God might sovereignly choose not to save his sons, and for Piper, it is a matter of piety to bow in adoration to such a God. Ironically, it even seems *Piper is more certain of his own desire to see his children saved than he is that God wills their salvation.*

While he thinks he would be willing to give his own life for the salvation of his sons, he thinks it is possible that God's glory might be shown forth most clearly in sovereignly choosing them for eternal damnation.

This may be Calvinist piety at its best, but it is deeply at odds with the biblical picture of a God who loves all his fallen children and seeks to save all who are lost. Jesus teaches us that God is like a good shepherd who is not content with the ninety-nine sheep he has safely at home, for his love continues to go out to the one that is lost. "I tell you that in the same way there will be more rejoicing in heaven over one sinner who repents than over ninety-nine righteous persons who do not need to repent" (Luke 15:7).

What truly glorifies God?

It is worth emphasizing here that N. T. Wright, the great evangelical New Testament scholar, has argued that Piper's account of the glory of God is deeply misguided. Indeed, Wright points out that

8. Piper, "How Does a Sovereign God Love? A Reply to Thomas Talbott," 13.

Piper's interpretation of the phrase "the righteousness of God" as God's concern for his own glory is a view that is peculiar to him, and not shared by any other biblical scholars.[9] More importantly, Wright argues that the truly biblical view of the glory of God runs in a very different direction than Piper thinks.

> He [Piper] sees it as God's concern for his own glory, which implies that God's primary concern returns, as it were, to himself. There is always a sense in which that is true. But the great story of Scripture, from creation and covenant right on through to the New Jerusalem, is constantly about God's overflowing, generous, creative love—God's concern, if you like, for the flourishing and well-being of everything else. Of course this too will redound to God's glory because God, as the Creator, is glorified when creation is flourishing and able to praise him gladly and freely. . . . God's concern for God's glory is precisely rescued from the appearance of divine narcissism because God, not least God as Trinity, is always giving out, pouring out, lavishing generous love on undeserving people, undeserving Israel and an undeserving world. That is the sort of God he is, and "God's righteousness" is a way of saying, "Yes, and God will be true to that character."[10]

How we understand what it means for God to be true to his character is one of the most revealing things about any system of theology. As Piper sees it, to be true to himself requires God to display the full range of his wrath, and this requires some persons to be eternally damned. By contrast, for Wright, God is the sort of God whose glory is

God is the sort of God whose glory is fully displayed in his generous love that he pours out on undeserving people

9. See Wright, *Justification*, 64ff.
10. Ibid., 70–71.

fully displayed in his generous love that he pours out on undeserving people.

In view of this, I find the following passage from Piper more than a little ironic.

> But is it loving for God to exalt his own glory? Yes it is. And there are several ways to see this truth clearly. One way is to ponder this sentence: *God is most glorified in us when we are most satisfied in him.* This is perhaps the most important sentence in my theology. If it is true, then it becomes plain why God is loving when he seeks to exalt his glory in my life. For that would mean that he would seek to maximize my satisfaction in him, since he is most glorified in me when I am most satisfied in him. . . . In fact it means that the more passionate God is for his own glory, the more passionate he is for my satisfaction in that glory.[11]

Notice what Piper says is perhaps the most important sentence in his theology: God is most glorified in us when we are most satisfied in him! But here is the question that screams for an answer: if this is so, why does God need to damn anyone by his sovereign choice in order for his full glory to be displayed? For the damned in hell are certainly *not* satisfied in God.

If God is MOST glorified in us when we are most satisfied in him, then it seems God should give everyone his irresistible grace, and cause all of them to experience the great satisfaction of salvation

So if God is MOST glorified in us when we are most satisfied in him, then it seems God should give everyone his irresistible grace, and cause all of them to experience the great satisfaction of salvation. That it seems would glorify God even more according to Piper's own claim that "God is most glorified in us when we are most satisfied in him."

11. Piper, *Let the Nations Be Glad!* 26.

In any case, Piper's conviction that God must sovereignly choose to damn some persons to be true to himself and to fully glorify himself is yet another instance of the same pattern we have observed. That is, Calvinists are so dazzled by the power of God that they invariably end up denying or distorting the love of God.

Piper's attempt to claim that God loves all persons, like that of Carson, is hollow indeed when we examine carefully just what they mean by that claim. This is a most telling sign that something is deeply wrong at the heart of Calvinism.

PART II

God Is Love

CHAPTER 6

A Theology of True Love

LET US TURN NOW to consider a theology that is much more faithful to the biblical vision of a God whose eternal nature is love. Here it is important to emphasize that Calvinism is very much a minority position in the history of Christian theology, even though it is a very vocal and influential minority position. It is certainly true that many noted theologians and preachers have been Calvinists, but the fact remains that in the church at large, Calvinists are, and always have been, a distinct minority. So there are many theologians who could be cited in sketching a theology of true love that does justice to biblical vision of God, but I will begin with Jacob Arminius (1560–1609), the great Dutch theologian who was born in the sixteenth century.

Arminius

Arminius, of course, is the person after whom Arminian theology is named, just as Calvin is the person after whom Calvinism is named. But the earlier source of "Calvinism" is St. Augustine, who lived many centuries before Calvin, and influenced many later theologians, both Protestant and Roman Catholic. Likewise, there were many early church fathers who held essentially the same theology as Arminius many centuries before he lived. But both systems of theology have come to be named after these famous theologians of the sixteenth century because each of them gave powerful expression to their systems of theology.

A foundation of love

Here is the point I want to emphasize that will be central to this chapter. Arminian theology is founded squarely on a strong account of the love of God. Unlike Calvinism, which often has a blind spot about God's love, Arminian theology stresses that God's love is absolutely foundational for a true account of Christian theology. Consider these telling words of Arminius.

> Considered as a whole, the foundation of the Christian faith is rooted in the twofold love of God, without which there neither is nor can be any [Christian] religion. The first is love of justice, which is the source of God's hatred of sin. The second is the love for humanity, endowed by God with reason.[1]

As Arminius sees it, the love of God is so central to Christianity that Christianity could not possibly exist without it. The love of God is not a secondary truth that might be overlooked or given a relatively minor emphasis compared to sovereignty or power. Quite to the contrary, for Arminius, without the love of God, there is no Christianity.

For Arminius, without the love of God, there is no Christianity

This love of God that is absolutely essential for Arminius is a twofold reality. The first aspect of this love of God is his love of justice. Arminius describes this as follows.

> The love of justice, on which the Christian religion rests, is, first, that justice which God declared once and for all in Christ. It was God's will that sin would not be forgiven in any other way than by the blood and death of his Son, and that Christ would not come before Him in any other way as advocate and intercessor except when sprinkled by his own blood.[2]

1. Arminius, *Arminius and His Declaration of Sentiments*, 124.
2. Ibid., 125.

God loves justice because he rightly loves himself, the ultimate source and ground of justice. So to be true himself, he *cannot* ever act unjustly. God's plan of salvation, then, will be true to his justice, according to Arminius. This brings us to the second part of the twofold love of God.

> The second point of the twofold love, on which the Christian faith is founded, is God's love for miserable sinners, that love by which he gave his Son for them and constituted Christ as Savior of those who are obedient to him. This love for sinners and the required obedience does not rest on the rigor and severity to which God is supremely entitled, but according to his grace and mercy.[3]

God's love for miserable sinners is what moves him to provide salvation for them. God's heart of love for his fallen children flows out of his perfect nature just as surely as his love of justice.

Now here it is crucial to emphasize that everything that is distinctively Christian about our faith is whatever has been revealed by the life, death, and resurrection of Christ. *Christianity* is what it is because of *Christ*. Notice that both aspects of the twofold love of God are shown to us through Christ.

First, God shows his love for justice "once and for all in Christ." God chooses to forgive sins through the atoning sacrifice of Christ in which he bled and died to reconcile us to God. Second, we see God's love for miserable sinners in his gift of Christ for our salvation and his offer of forgiveness to all who repent. So in short, when we see Christ dying on the cross, we see a

When we see Christ dying on the cross, we see a vivid picture of the twofold love of God. We see both God's love of justice and his heart of love for his fallen children

3. Ibid., 125–26.

vivid picture of the twofold love of God. We see both God's love of justice and his heart of love for his fallen children.

Now then, let us turn to consider the Arminian account of those central doctrines we have examined in Calvinism. Whereas Calvinists teach limited atonement only for the elect, Arminians teach that Christ truly died for all. Whereas Calvinists teach unconditional election, Arminians teach that election is conditional. And whereas Calvinists teach that God's saving grace is irresistible, Arminians teach that grace can be resisted.[4]

Let us look at each of these key doctrines in order.

Christ truly died for all

Perhaps nothing brings more starkly into focus profound differences between Calvinist and Arminian theology than their very different answers to this question: for whom did Christ die? As we have seen, Calvinist theology holds the view that is commonly known as "limited atonement," which is the view that Christ died only for those that God has chosen unconditionally to save, or at least he died for them in a different sense than he did for the elect. The rest of mankind are those that God has chosen by his sovereign will to pass over and condemn to eternal damnation. Christ did not die to save these persons, and none of them will receive his irresistible grace.

Arminian theology . . . insists in the strongest possible terms that because God deeply loves ALL persons, Christ truly died for ALL

4. Recall the Arminian acronym cited earlier:
Freed by grace (to believe)
Atonement for all
Conditional election
Total Depravity
Security in Christ

Arminian theology, by contrast, insists in the strongest possible terms that because God deeply loves ALL persons, Christ truly died for ALL. The gospel is truly good news for the whole world, including every person who has been, or ever will be born. "For God so loved *the world* that he gave his only Son, that everyone who believes in him may not perish but have eternal life" (John 3:16). And in the very first chapter of John, we read: "The next day he [John the Baptist] saw Jesus coming toward him and declared, 'Here is the lamb of God who takes away the sin of *the world*'" (John 1:29; see also John 4:42; 6:51).

Calvinists, of course, argue that "the world" does not literally mean every person in the world in these passages. It means only that Christ died for *all kinds of people* all over the world, but not every individual. Arminians, along with many other Christians, find these interpretations highly artificial, and think it is clear that God's love as expressed in Christ is truly extended to all people.

The fact that Christ died for all is stated even more clearly in the First Epistle of John: "and he [Jesus Christ] is the atoning sacrifice for our sins, and not for ours only but also for the sins of the whole world" (1 John 2:2; see also 4:14; Heb 2:9). Notice: *he did not die for our sins only, but for the sins of the whole world.* Here it is very difficult for Calvinists to argue that "the world" means "the elect, composed of all kinds of people from all over the world" because the "world" is *distinguished* from the Christ-believing audience of the letter. Here "the world" means "all those who are *not* currently a part of the Christian community."

Now let us turn to the Epistles of Paul, where we also see some powerful statements that Christ truly died for all persons. In Romans, Paul addresses his fellow believers and urges them to avoid doing things that will cause others to stumble. In particular, eating certain kinds of meat at that time could be considered wrong, and would offend the conscience of some persons. In view of that, Paul wrote: "Do not let what you eat be the ruin of one for whom Christ died" (Rom 14:15; see also 2 Pet 2:1). What is noteworthy here is that Paul considers the possibility that weaker persons might be spiritually ruined in this situation, but Paul is still confident that Christ died for them.

Another striking text in Romans that bears on this issue is the following: "Therefore, just as one man's trespass led to condemnation for all, so one man's act of righteousness leads to justification for *all*" (Rom 5:18). What is particularly telling here is the parallel between the sin of Adam, which led to condemnation for "all" and the obedience of Christ (all the way to the cross) that provides justification for "all." Now clearly, "all" in the case of Adam includes every individual, so there is every reason to think the "all" in the case of Christ does too.

Consider in the same vein this text from the Apostle Paul.

> For the love of Christ urges us on, because we are convinced that *one has died for all*; therefore all have died. And he died for all, so that those who live might live no longer for themselves, but for him who died and was raised for them. (2 Cor 5:14-15)

Notice that Christ died and was raised for all of us so that we might live no longer for ourselves, but for him. He died for all of us so that all of us might live for him!

Paul continues a few verses later to spell out how this shapes his ministry. Indeed, the death of Christ for all is the basis for his ministry of reconciliation.

> All this is from God, who reconciled us to himself through Christ, and has given us the ministry of reconciliation: that is, *in Christ God was reconciling the world to himself*, not counting their trespasses against them, and entrusting the message of reconciliation to us. So we are ambassadors for Christ, since God is making his appeal through us; we entreat you on behalf of Christ, be reconciled to God. (2 Cor 5:18-20)

God reconciled the world to himself through Christ, and now he is making his appeal through his ambassadors to accept the reconciliation that is offered. He died for *all* and the appeal goes out to *all:* "be reconciled to God!"

The universal nature of the atonement is also an important theme in Paul's "pastoral epistles," his letters to Timothy and Titus. One of the most famous verses in all of Scripture that affirms God's will to provide salvation for all persons appears in these pastoral epistles: "[God] *desires everyone to be saved* and to come to the knowledge of the truth" (1 Tim 2:4). It is most significant that Paul continues as follows.

> For there is one God; there is also one mediator between God and humankind, Christ Jesus, himself human, who gave himself *a ransom for all*—this was attested at the right time. (1 Tim 2:5–6)

Later on, Paul reiterates this vital truth when he writes that "we have set our hope on the living God, who is the Savior of *all people*, especially of those who believe" (1 Tim 4:10; see also Titus 2:11). This is the good news of the gospel. There is one mediator between God and man, Jesus Christ "who gave himself *a ransom for all*." He is the Savior of all people, and he urges all to believe and accept the salvation he has so richly provided.

Again, it is a very telling window into Calvinist theology that Calvinists take pains to try to show these verses do not in fact teach what they so clearly seem to teach. Calvinists are determined to deny that Christ truly died for all in order to defend their claim that God has chosen to restrict his grace and salvation to those he has unconditionally elected to save, consigning the rest to eternal damnation.

Election is conditional

A common caricature you sometimes hear is that Calvinists believe in predestination and election, whereas Arminians believe in free will. And whereas Calvinists believe God is sovereign, Arminians end up making man sovereign over a helpless God. The truth of the matter, however, is altogether different from this simplistic caricature. The reality is that both Arminians and Calvinists believe in predestination and election, and they both believe in free will, but they understand these things very differently. Likewise, Arminians also heartily affirm the sovereignty of God, but they have a very different account of sovereignty than Calvinists do.

Arminius, in fact, gave extensive attention to the doctrines of predestination and election and affirmed a very strong account of those doctrines, which anyone who takes the time to read Arminius himself can easily see.[5] John Wesley (1703–91), founder of Methodism, also had a strong view of these doctrines that emphasized the love and goodness of God. So let us consider Wesley's account to see how radically different it is from that of Calvinism.

---

5. For an account of his views on these issues, see Arminius, *Arminius and His Declaration of Sentiments*, 103–39.

Wesley

A concise account of his view appears in his sermon "On Predestination," for which he chose a classic text dealing with this great biblical truth, namely, Romans 8:29–30.

> For whom he did foreknow, he also did predestinate to be conformed to the image of his Son, that he might be the firstborn among many brethren. Moreover whom he did predestinate, them he also called: and whom he called, them he also justified: and whom he justified, them he also glorified. (KJV)

A Theology of True Love

Here Paul summarizes God's action in saving us in terms of his foreknowing us, predestining us, calling us, justifying us, and glorifying us. As Wesley notes, some have understood this text as a "chain of causes and effects," but he argues that it simply shows *"the method in which God works—the order* in which the several branches of salvation constantly flow from each other."[6]

But again, it is important to stress that Wesley insists on a very strong doctrine of predestination. Here are some lines from his sermon that capture the heart of his view.

> God decrees from everlasting to everlasting that all who believe in the Son of his love shall be conformed to his image, shall be saved from all inward and outward sin into all inward and outward holiness . . . and this in virtue of the unchangeable, irreversible, irresistible decree of God: "He that believeth shall be saved; he that believeth not shall be damned."[7]

Notice, God has decreed from all eternity who will be saved: namely, those who believe in Jesus, the Son of his love. His eternal decree, moreover, is irreversible and irresistible. God sets the terms of salvation and those terms are unalterable. There is no other way to be saved. Furthermore, God has decreed that those who believe in Jesus are predestined to be conformed to his image, to become holy, through and through, just like Jesus is.

Predestination is like a train that has a pre-determined destination. All who board the train and remain on it will inevitably arrive at that pre-determined destination

6. Wesley, *The Works of John Wesley*, Vol. 2, 416. For a more detailed discussion, see Wesley's essay "Predestination Calmly Considered" in *The Works of John Wesley*, Vol. 13, 261–320.

7. Wesley, *The Works of John Wesley*, Vol. 2, 418.

A train bound for heaven

Think of it this way. Predestination is like a train that has a pre-determined destination. All who board the train and remain on it will inevitably arrive at that pre-determined destination. Moreover, there is no other way to reach that destination. If we want to make it there, we have to get on that train, and remain on it through each of the stops along the way. The train is firmly on the track, and the engineer is fully capable and determined to bring all passengers who are aboard to the pre-determined destination.

The predetermined destination is heaven; it is holiness; it is being like Jesus. And the only way we can get there is through faith in Jesus. In fact, we might even say that Jesus is the train. The call of God invites us to board the train. If we exercise faith in Christ, we are "in Christ" as Paul puts it (Eph 1:3–14). And all who are "in Christ" are on the way to the predestined end so long as they stay on the train. Those who are called to believe, to "come aboard," may choose not to do so, and if they decide they do not want to be made holy like Jesus, they may exit the train at one of its stops along the way.

Here we see a parting of the ways between the classical Arminian view of predestination, as represented by Wesley, and the Calvinist view. We can put the question like this: who can get on the train? As we have seen, the Calvinist answer is that the only ones who can actually get on are the unconditionally elect who receive the effectual call, and God's irresistible grace. The Wesleyan/Arminian answer is that everyone is not only invited and called to get on, but that God gives everyone the grace that actually enables them to do so. God's grace both calls us to believe, *and* enables us to do so. God has "purchased a ticket" for everyone, and our part is merely to exercise faith and accept the gift of salvation. Paul famously put it like this in describing how we are saved: "For by grace you have been saved through faith, and this is not of your own doing; it is the gift of God—not the result of works, so that no one may boast" (Eph 2:8–9).[8]

When we exercise faith, we are "in Christ," and we are accordingly on the train that is predestined to eternal salvation. If we refuse to believe, we remain outside of Christ, who is the only way to salvation. In so refusing, we reject the ticket to salvation that God has purchased for us.

"Unsearchable" will and voluntarism

Wesley strongly emphasized that the conditional view of predestination is true to God's character as a God of perfect love, goodness, and justice. Recall that the Calvinist view of predestination emphasizes God's sovereign power and the "unsearchable counsel of his own will, whereby he extendeth or withholdeth mercy as he pleaseth."

The notion that God's sovereign will in predestination is "unsearchable" reminds us of the fact that Calvinism often reflects the worst tendencies of extreme voluntarism. Extreme voluntarism is the notion that God could will anything, and his willing it would make it right. God could will lying, rape, even blasphemy, and if he chose to will these things, then they would be right, and we would be required to do them. God's sovereign will is "unsearchable" in the sense that he can will things that make no moral or rational sense to us what-

> *Extreme voluntarism: God could will lying, rape, even blasphemy, and if he chose to will these things, then they would be right, and we would be required to do them*

8. Calvinists sometimes claim that even our faith is a gift in the sense that it is caused or determined by God, and not a free response. For a discussion of this text that shows why the Arminian interpretation makes better sense of the original Greek, see my *Why I am Not a Calvinist*, 75–79.

soever. The notion that God's sovereign will is "unsearchable" in this sense is for Calvinists an essential part of his glory.

Now it is one thing to say, "whatever God wills is right," but it is another thing altogether to say "God can will anything and make it right." I would agree with the former statement. Anything God wills is surely right. But it does not follow that God can will literally anything and make it right. There are some things God cannot do, and the fact that he cannot do them is a reflection of his almighty power and his perfect character, not of weakness. God cannot lie, he cannot fail to keep his promises, he cannot be untrue to himself, and he cannot do anything that would be inconsistent with his perfect love.

Consider an example. I do not believe I am capable of strangling my little granddaughters. Does this show that I am weak or does it reflect negatively on me that I cannot do this? No, surely not! It is not because I lack the physical strength, but because I love them dearly. In the same way, there are things God cannot do because of his character of perfect love and goodness.[9] He cannot do them *because* he is perfect.

"Unsearchable" will versus "known" rules of justice and mercy

By sharp contrast, Wesley thought Calvinist theology fundamentally mistaken to emphasize God's "unsearchable" sovereignty as the explanation for why some persons are saved and others are lost. He argued that in the matter of salvation, "God proceeds according to the known rules of his justice and mercy."[10] Notice: Wesley emphasizes God's "known" rules of justice and mercy, rather than his "unsearchable" or "secret" will. In other words, Wesley insisted that God has revealed the terms of salvation, so

9. For more on Calvinism and voluntarism, see Baggett and Walls, *Good God*, 73–75; Walls, "Divine Commands, Predestination, and Moral Intuition."

10. Wesley, *The Works of John Wesley*, Vol. 13, 277.

that predestination and election are not a matter of utter mystery. To the contrary, the terms God has revealed make rational and moral sense. Wesley elaborated on this point as follows.

> But in disposing the eternal states of men . . . it is clear, that not sovereignty alone, but justice, mercy, and truth hold the reins. The Governor of heaven and earth, the I AM, over all, God blessed forever, takes no step here but as these direct, and prepare the way before his face. This is his eternal and irresistible will as he hath revealed unto us by his Spirit; declaring in the strongest terms, adding his oath to his word, and because he could swear by no greater, swearing by himself, "As I live, saith the Lord God, I have no pleasure in the death of him that dieth." "The death of him that dieth can never be resolved into my pleasure or sovereign will." No; it is impossible.[11]

The doctrine of conditional election makes sense of the profound biblical truth that God takes no pleasure in the death of the wicked. The reason why anyone is lost is entirely due to *their own* choice, and the fact that they have rejected God's gracious offer of salvation, which they really could have accepted, but persistently refused. Wesley spelled out God's offer of salvation in very strong terms. God's loving mercy is displayed, he wrote, " in offering salvation to every creature, actually saving all that consent thereto, and doing for the rest all that infinite wisdom, almighty power, and boundless love can do, without *forcing* them to be saved, which would be to destroy the very nature that he had given them."[12]

> *The reason why anyone is lost is entirely due to their own choice, and the fact that they have rejected God's gracious offer of salvation, which they really could have accepted, but persistently refused*

11. Ibid., 293–94; see also 548–50.
12. Ibid., 393.

Does God Love Everyone?

Wesley believed that God so thoroughly pours out his love on all persons that he can say them, "What could I have done for you which I have not done?" (see Isa 5:4).[13] Now if election is unconditional and grace is irresistible, the sinner might well answer, "You could have given me the irresistible grace you gave those persons you elected for salvation, but that you withheld from me." Wesley, by contrast, believes sinners will have no answer to God's question in Isaiah 5:4.

The conditional view of election not only shows forth God's love more clearly, but also his justice. Here are two key reasons. First, it shows he treats like cases alike. On the Calvinist view, of course, God does not treat like cases alike. He sovereignly chooses to spare some sinners, but condemns others who are no more worthy of punishment than those who are saved. On the conditional view of election, God truly loves all persons and gives all of them every opportunity to be saved. Those who accept his grace are saved, and those who reject his grace are lost.

Second, since those who reject grace do so freely, they are not condemned for sins they could not possibly have avoided committing. By contrast, those who are predestined for hell on the Calvinist view could not avoid the sins they commit since they cannot possibly accept Christ without the irresistible grace God chooses not to give them. Wesley believed that is obviously unjust to punish such persons.

"*He will punish no man for doing anything which he could not possibly avoid, neither for omitting anything which he could not possibly do*"

He will punish no man for doing anything which he could not possibly avoid, neither for omitting anything which he could not possibly do. Every punishment supposes the offender might have avoided the offense for which he is punished. Otherwise to punish him would

13. Ibid., 291.

be palpably unjust, and inconsistent with the character of God our Governor.[14]

The conditional view of election, then, shows forth not only God's love for all persons, but also his justice. It makes rational and moral sense by appealing to the "known" principles of God's mercy and justice rather than to the sheer mystery of his "secret" or "unsearchable" sovereign will to explain why some persons are saved, but others are lost.

Does our free response diminish God's glory?

Before concluding our discussion of conditional election, we should consider a common Calvinist criticism. Conditional election, they say, detracts from the glory of God and his grace because it makes *us* the decisive factor in our salvation rather than God. According to John Piper, for example, Arminians believe that "whatever other influences may lead toward a decision, the influence that settles the choice is the human self."[15]

This claim, however, misrepresents the Arminian view. What we need to see here is that our free choice plays a much different role in salvation than it does in damnation. It is certainly true that our free consent, our faith, is a necessary condition for our salvation. (Indeed, Calvinists typically agree that faith is a necessary condition for salvation, but they think faith is determined by God rather than being a free choice on our part.) However, what needs to be emphasized is that *God's grace always takes the initiative and enables our free response.* Moreover, it is his ongoing grace in our life that leads to our sanctification

God's grace always takes the initiative and enables our free response

14. Ibid., 550.
15. Piper, *Does God Desire All to Be Saved?* 40. See also 15n.5 and 53.

and final salvation. Consider this chart that depicts the role of our free response in our salvation.

Created in God's image (so only God can satisfy) →

Christ died for us →

The Holy Spirit draws us (prevenient grace) →

Our free response of faith →

Regeneration and justification →

Our free cooperation →

Sanctification →

→ → → → → → → Glorification and final salvation

Notice all the large arrows that represent God's action and God's initiative in our salvation. By contrast, notice the small arrows that represent our free response of faith and our cooperation in our sanctification. Certainly our free response is a necessary condition for our salvation, but it is clear that God plays the decisive role. He not only initiates things, he also does the decisive act of regenerating us, and then sanctifying us in response to our faith. He is the one who finally glorifies us and seals our final salvation. So it is clear that it is the gracious action of God that finally settles things, and *not us*.

The role of human free choice in damnation is another matter altogether, however. To see the difference, compare this chart with the previous one.

Created in God's image (so only God can satisfy) →

Christ died for us →

The Holy Spirit draws us (prevenient grace) →

Freely resisting grace ←←

Ongoing grace and divine love →

Persistent rebellion and unbelief ←←

Damnation ←←←←

Notice that in this chart, *human free choice is the decisive factor in damnation.* The choice to resist grace and to persist in rebellion and unbelief is what leads decisively to damnation. So long as we continue to hold on to our sin rather than to repent and accept God's freely offered gifts of forgiveness and regeneration, we remain separated from God. It is entirely the free human choice to reject God's grace that leads to damnation.

But the question may still persist of how human beings can resist a sovereign God. Doesn't this make God weak somehow? If grace can be resisted, doesn't this still impugn the glory of God? Let us now turn to the doctrine that grace is resistible grace to answer this question.

Human free choice is the decisive factor in damnation

Resistible grace

As we saw in chapter 4, Jacob Arminius thought this was the big issue that divided him from Calvinism. He put it like this, you may remember: "The entire controversy can be reduced to answering this question, 'Is the grace of God an irresistible force?'" Recall also this passage from Calvin in chapter 3:

> I, at least, maintain this teaching of Augustine's: where
> God makes sheep out of wolves, he reforms them by a
> more powerful grace to subdue their hardness; accord-
> ingly, God does not convert the obstinate because he
> does not manifest that more powerful grace, which is
> not lacking if he should please to offer it.

And finally recall the passage from the *Westminster Confession
of Faith* describing the "effectual call." It says God acts "by his
almighty power, determining them to that which is good." Now
notice the thought in both Calvin and the *Westminster Confession:* grace is presented as a product of God's almighty power,
and as such, it cannot be resisted. God can subdue any stubborn
wolf he wishes and turn him or her into a sheep by exercising his
supreme power.

It's not a power play

Now if grace is a power play between God and humans, then
surely it is irresistible. Let me be very clear. If it is a simple question of *power*, the sort of power God exerted when he created our
massive universe, or raised Jesus from the dead, then *God can
determine anyone to do anything he wants them to do.* God can
move my body any way he wants, he can move my tongue and lips
to speak any words he wants me to speak, he can cause me to feel
anything he wants me to feel. He can cause me to profess him as
Lord, and to say the words "I love you, Father."

God wants us to respond to him with genuine love . . . and such love cannot be caused or determined simply by an exercise of sovereign power

But this is exactly what is wrong
with this picture. God does not come to
us to simply in omnipotent power when
he offers his grace to us. He comes to
us in *love,* and he wants us to respond
to him with genuine love, trust, and

obedience. And such love cannot be caused or determined simply by an exercise of sovereign power.

Of course, love is a very powerful thing in another sense of the word. When love touches our hearts it has transforming power. It inspires and moves us to want to return the love we have been shown. Consider the final two verses of Isaac Watts' famous hymn, "When I Survey the Wondrous Cross" in which he contemplates the amazing love of God as shown in the death of Christ on a bloody cross.

> See from His head, His hands, His feet,
> Sorrow and love flow mingled down!
> Did e'er such love and sorrow meet,
> Or thorns compose so rich a crown?
>
> Were the whole realm of nature mine,
> That were a present far too small;
> Love so amazing, so divine,
> Demands my soul, my life, my all.

Sacrificial love is a powerful thing and it "demands" a response of love from the persons who are given this wonderful gift. But the "demand" is not that of a mighty monarch wearing a crown of gold and bearing a sword. It is the demand of the King who comes to us "gentle and humble of heart" (Matt 11:28–30) wearing a crown of thorns. This is a different kind of power than the sort of power that is expressed in a display of great strength or an impressive show of authority.

God's nature and our free response

God is love *in his very nature*, as we saw in chapter 1. And he is love in his very nature because he is the Trinity, and there has been love among the three Persons of the Trinity from all eternity.

He created us in his image for a relationship with himself and with other persons, and since he is love in his very nature, those relationships will be relationships of love. Recall the following verses from John's Gospel that I cited, and the remarkable connection between them, but now let's add another verse:

> "Father . . . you loved me before the creation of the world" (John 17:24)

> "As the Father has loved me, so have I loved you" (John 15:9)

> "My command is this: Love each other as I have loved you" (John 15:12)

Now these extraordinary words from Jesus are even more amazing in light of the two previous verses. Jesus loves us as the Father has loved him from all eternity, and he now calls us to love each other *as he loves us!* Think about that! Jesus calls us to love each other in a way that resembles the eternal love between the Father, Son, and Holy Spirit. *Our love for each other should mirror the Trinity!*

But notice this also. While the first two verses state objective facts, the third verse comes to us as a command. And commands require free obedience. Implicit in the command is the possibility that we will choose to disobey what Jesus directs us to do. While God is love in his very nature, and cannot fail to love, finite beings created in his image must freely choose to love and obey God in order to become fully loving beings.[16] Consider in this light another passage from John.

> Jesus replied, "If anyone loves me, he will obey my teaching. My Father will love him, and we will come to

---

16. See Rasmussen, "On the Value of Freedom to do Evil" and Timpe, *Free Will in Philosophical Theology*, 103–18.

him and make our home with him. He who does not
love me will not obey my teaching." (John 14:23–24a)

Again, the point here is that love requires a free response.
Jesus seeks those who will love him and obey his teaching, and he
offers the greatest possible gifts for those who do so. His Father
will love those who obey Jesus, and both he and Jesus with make
their home with those persons. What an amazing thought! The
Father and Son want to love us, and make their home with us!
They want to be at home with us in a relationship of mutual love
that mirrors the eternal love of the Trinity.

But the astounding possibility that still remains is that some
persons may not love Jesus or obey his teaching. And they may
reject the offer of the greatest relationship possible. God wants
to come into their lives and be at home with him, but they may
choose to keep him out. Hear now these words addressed by Jesus
to the church in Laodicea.

> You say, "I am rich; I have acquired wealth and do
> not need a thing." But you do not realize that you are
> wretched, pitiful, poor, blind, and naked. I counsel you
> to buy from me gold refined in the fire, so you can be-
> come rich; and white clothes to wear, so you can cover
> your shameful nakedness; and salve to put on your eyes
> so you can see. Those whom I love I rebuke and disci-
> pline. So be earnest and repent. Here I am! I stand at the
> door and knock. If anyone hears my voice and opens
> the door, I will come in and eat with him, and he with
> me. (Rev 3:17–20)

Once again, the Lord of the Universe comes with the offer
of priceless gifts. He offers refined gold in place of poverty, white
clothes in place of shameful nakedness, sight instead of blindness.
He offers to come in and eat us, and to make himself at home with
us.

But marvel of marvels, the Almighty Lord of the Universe
stands outside and knocks. He comes with encouragement to

accept his gifts and with loving discipline. He patiently counsels, he graciously rebukes, he persistently knocks and offers to come in. But he does not exert his almighty power to break open the door.

Love is stronger than hate, it is stronger than evil, even stronger than death. But amazing as it is, love can still be rejected

The invitation of love is not a contest of strength or sheer power. God's love cannot be defeated or overcome. As I noted in chapter 1, love is stronger than hate, it is stronger than evil, even stronger than death. But amazing as it is, love can still be rejected. And that is perhaps the deepest reason why grace is not irresistible.

Conclusion

IN CHAPTER 1 OF this book, I quoted Question 4 of *The Shorter Catechism* of the *Westminster Confession of Faith*. "What is God?" is the question, you may recall, and here is the answer: "God is a Spirit, infinite, eternal, and unchangeable, in his being, wisdom, power, holiness, justice, goodness, and truth." We noted that this definition leaves out one of most beautiful truths about God's eternal, unchangeable being: "God is love."

Now compare this statement from *The Shorter Catechism* with the passage below from John Wesley. In this passage, Wesley is making the case that the Calvinist doctrines of unconditional election and reprobation are utterly inconsistent with what the Bible teaches about God. These doctrines, he argued, are inconsistent with God's justice, truth, and sincerity. Wesley went on to insist, however, that these Calvinist doctrines are even more at odds with another attribute of God.

> But do they not agree least of all with the scriptural account of his love and goodness? That attribute which God peculiarly claims, wherein he glories above all the rest. It is not written, "God is justice," or "God is truth" (although he is just and true in all his ways). But it is written, "God is love," love in the abstract, without bounds; and "There is no end of his goodness." His love extends even to those who neither love nor fear him. He

is good even to the evil and the unthankful; yea, without any exception or limitation, all the children of men. For "the Lord is loving" (or good) "to every man and his mercy is over all his works."[1]

That last verse that Wesley cited here is Psalm 145:9, which was one of his favorite texts. He began one of his sermons by quoting it as follows: "Nothing is more sure than that as 'the Lord is loving to every man,' so 'his mercy is over all his works'—all that have sense, all that are capable of pleasure or pain, of happiness and misery."[2]

One of the most telling things about any system of theology or philosophy is what it takes to be "most sure." What is it that is utterly clear and non-negotiable? For Wesley "nothing is more sure" than the fact that God is love, and that God sincerely and deeply loves all persons.

A stark contrast, and the heart of the issue

The contrast with Calvinism is stark. The text that Wesley thought most clearly defined God was not quoted even one time in Calvin's *Institutes*. The attribute *The Shorter Catechism* omitted from its list of divine attributes was the one Wesley thought "God peculiarly claims." Whereas Calvinists often argue that God would not be fully glorified if he did not sovereignly choose to damn some persons to eternal hell, Wesley thought that love was the attribute "wherein he glories above the rest."

Is God good in the sense that he deeply and sincerely loves all persons?

The deepest issue that divides Arminians and Calvinists is not the sovereignty of God, predestination, or the authority of the Bible. The deepest difference pertains to how we understand the character of God.

1. Wesley, *The Works of John Wesley*, Vol. 13, 284–85.
2. Ibid., Vol. 2, 437.

Is God good in the sense that he deeply and sincerely loves all persons?

That is the heart of the issue that Southern Baptists, Pentecostal churches such as the Assemblies of God, and other evangelicals struggling with this issue need to decide as they move forward. It is important to stress that there is more involved here than a clear sense of theological identity, as important as that is. There are enormous practical implications that we cannot avoid. In particular, what is at stake is our very understanding of the gospel, and how we shall preach the good news to a lost and dying world.

In short, the practical issue is this: do we truly believe that God loves all persons in such a way that we can honestly tell the unconverted that God loves them? Can we forthrightly announce to all the unconverted that Jesus died for them and urge them to be reconciled to God? Do we truly believe that God's heart of love goes out to all, and he longs to embrace and restore all his prodigal children who are living with the pigs? (Luke 15)

Do we truly believe that God loves all persons in such a way that we can honestly tell the unconverted that God loves them?

One of the hallmarks of Pentecostalism, like the Wesleyan and Holiness movements before it, is that it has reached many people with the gospel who may have been written off as hopeless cases. Southern Baptists too are noted for evangelistic zeal and a passion to share the gospel with the whole world. The results have been dramatic. Countless persons whose lives have seemed broken beyond repair have been transformed by the gospel, lovingly proclaimed by evangelists who delight in sharing the good news. Everyone from drug addicts to prostitutes to alcoholics to sex addicts have experienced the transforming love of God and have become powerful witnesses to his amazing grace.

So here is the question: is it even possible according to our theology that there is a single prostitute, drug addict, or violent criminal who is hopeless because God has sovereignly chosen to exclude him or her from salvation? Are any persons utterly hopeless because Jesus did not die for them or because God needs to damn them so he will be fully glorified? Or do we passionately believe that Jesus died for everyone, from the homeless drunk who begs on the street corner to the billionaire in his Ferrari? Do we truly believe not only that all need salvation, but that salvation is genuinely offered and available to all? *That* is the issue.

Perhaps the point I am making can be seen most clearly if we consider the famous statue of Jesus called "Christ the Redeemer" that looks over the city of Rio de Janeiro, Brazil. In this statue, Christ's arms are open wide, as if to beckon all to come to him for salvation. A picture of this statue appears, ironically, on the cover of John Piper's little book *Does God Desire All to Be Saved?* As I read Piper's book, I could not help but think what a misleading image that is, given his explanation of how God loves those he has chosen for damnation.

Rio

Indeed, I think a better image of the Calvinist view of the love of God would be Christ with one arm extended in love, but with his other arm behind his back, with his fingers "secretly" crossed. Calvinism simply cannot make coherent sense of God's love for all persons and it would be better to forthrightly admit that, than to maintain a posture of love for all that is utterly hollow when carefully examined.

Southern Baptists are clearly committed to making room for both views, and that makes sense for them, given their history. Pentecostal churches, however, are another matter, given the Wesleyan roots of most Pentecostal theology. The question they need to answer is whether they are truly committed to a robust view of the love of God, and want to proclaim this forthrightly and without equivocation.

They too may choose to follow the same course as the Southern Baptists, and leave this matter open, or remain neutral or ambiguous in their theological commitments. But if they truly believe Christ died for all, and that God deeply loves all persons and is willing to save all of them, they should clearly and consistently affirm Arminian/Wesleyan theology.

Further Reading

Abasciano, Brian J. *Paul's Use of the Old Testament in Romans 9:1–9: An Intertextual and Theological Exegesis.* London: T. & T. Clark, 2006. (This volume is the first of three that provide an exhaustive analysis and commentary on this controversial passage of scripture. The second volume, which covers verses 10–18 was published in 2013; and the third, which covers verses 19–33, was published in 2015).

Collins, Kenneth J. *The Scripture Way of Salvation: The Heart of John Wesley's Theology.* Nashville: Abingdon, 1997.

———. *The Theology of John Wesley: Holy Love and the Shape of Grace.* Nashville: Abingdon, 2007.

Olson, Roger E. *Against Calvinism.* Grand Rapids: Zondervan, 2011.

———. *Arminian Theology: Myths and Realities.* Downers Grove, IL: IVP Academic, 2006.

Peckham, John C. *The Love of God: A Canonical Model.* Downers Grove, IL: IVP Academic, 2015.

Pinnock, Clark E., ed. *The Grace of God and the Will of Man.* Minneapolis: Bethany House, 1989.

Stanglin, Keith D., and Thomas McCall. *Jacob Arminius: Theologian of Grace.* New York: Oxford University Press, 2012.

Timpe, Kevin. *Free Will in Philosophical Theology.* New York: Bloomsbury, 2014.

Thorsen, Don. *Calvin vs. Wesley: Bringing Belief in Line with Practice.* Nashville: Abingdon, 2013.

Walls, Jerry L., and Joseph R. Dongell. *Why I am Not a Calvinist.* Downers Grove, IL: IVP, 2004.

———. "Why No Classical Theist, Let Alone Orthodox Christian, Should Ever Be a Compatibilist." *Philosophia Christi* 13 (2011), 75–104.

Witherington, Ben, and Darlene Hyatt. *Paul's Letter to the Romans: A Socio-Rhetorical Commentary.* Grand Rapids: Eerdmans, 2004.

Bibliography of Works Cited

Abasciano, Brian, and Martin Glynn. "An Outline of the FACTS of Arminianism vs. the TULIP of Calvinism. Online: http://evangelicalarminians.org/an-outline-of-the-facts-of-arminianism-vs-the-tulip-of-calvinism/.

"AG Position Papers and Other Statements." Online: http://ag.org/top/Beliefs/Position_Papers/.

Arminius, Jacob. *Arminius and his Declaration of Sentiments: An Annotated Translation with Introduction and Theological Commentary.* Translation, introduction, and commentary by Stephen W. Gunther. Waco, TX: Baylor University Press, 2012.

Baggett, David, and Jerry L. Walls. *Good God: The Theistic Foundations of Morality.* New York: Oxford University Press, 2011.

Barna Group. "Is There a 'Reformed' Movement in American Churches?" Online: https://www.barna.org/barna-update/faith-spirituality/447-reformed-movement-in-american-churches#.VtgUaBisTbG.

Calvin, John. *Institutes of the Christian Religion.* Edited by John T. McNeill. Translated by Ford Lewis Battles. Philadelphia: Westminster, 1960.

Carson, D. A. *The Difficult Doctrine of the Love of God.* Wheaton, IL: Crossway, 2000.

Dayton, Donald W. *Theological Roots of Pentecostalism.* Grand Rapids: Baker Academic, 1987.

Kinlaw, Dennis F., with John N. Oswalt. *Lectures in Old Testament Theology.* Anderson, IN: Francis Asbury, 2010.

Lewis, C. S. *Mere Christianity.* San Francisco: HarperSanFrancisco, 2001.

McCall, Thomas H. "We Believe in God's Sovereign Goodness: A Rejoinder to John Piper." *Trinity Journal* 29.2 (2008) 235–46.

Mohler, Albert. "Truth, Trust, and Testimony in a Time of Tension—The SBC and Its Future." Online: http://www.albertmohler.com/2013/06/11/truth-trust-and-testimony-in-a-time-of-tension-the-sbc-and-its-future/.

Olson, Roger E. *Arminian Theology: Myths and Realities.* Downers Grove, IL: IVP Academic, 2006.

Bibliography of Works Cited

———. "My Response to 'An Assemblies of God Response to Reformed Theology.'" Online: http://www.patheos.com/blogs/rogereolson/2015/11/ my-response-to-an-assemblies-of-god-response-to-reformed-theology/.

Pink, Arthur W. *The Sovereignty of God.* [1929] 3rd ed. Pensacola, FL: Chapel Library, 1999.

Piper, John. *Does God Desire All to Be Saved?* Wheaton, IL: Crossway, 2013.

———. "How Does a Sovereign God Love? A Reply to Thomas Talbott." *The Reformed Journal* 33.4 (1983) 9–13.

———. *Let the Nations Be Glad!* Grand Rapids: Baker, 1993.

Rasmussen, Joshua. "On the Value of Freedom to do Evil." *Faith and Philosophy* 30 (2013) 418–28.

Scroggins, Jimmy. "Truth, Trust, and Testimony in a Time of Tension." *SBC Life: Journal of the Southern Baptist Convention.* Online: http://www. sbclife.net/Articles/2013/06/sla5.

Thorson, Don. *Calvin vs. Wesley: Bringing Belief in Line with Practice.* Nashville: Abingdon, 2013.

Timpe, Kevin. *Free Will in Philosophical Theology.* New York: Bloomsbury, 2014.

Walls, Jerry L. "Divine Commands, Predestination, and Moral Intuition." In *The Grace of God and the Will of Man,* edited by Clark Pinnock, 261–76. Minneapolis: Bethany House, 1989.

Walls, Jerry L., and Joseph R. Dongell. *Why I am Not a Calvinist.* Downers Grove, IL: IVP, 2004.

Wesley, John. *The Works of John Wesley,* Vol. 2. Edited by Albert C. Outler. Nashville: Abingdon, 1985.

———. *The Works of John Wesley,* Vol. 13. Edited by Paul Wesley Chilcote and Kenneth J. Collins. Nashville: Abingdon, 2013.

The Westminster Confession of Faith. Online: http://www.reformed.org/ documents/wcf_with_proofs/.

Wright, N. T. *Justification: God's Plan & Paul's Vision.* Downers Grove, IL: IVP Academic, 2009.

Made in the USA
Coppell, TX
20 April 2021